PRAISE FOR *STORY 10X*

"*Story 10x* teaches a new kind of storytelling for startups in hyper-growth. A must read!"

VENETIA PRISTAVEC, FORMER CREATIVE DIRECTOR, AIRBNB

"Product managers need internal 'narratives' for their teams to conceptualize their products and goals. Especially when you're solving real people problems on a massive scale. The strategies in *Story 10x* dramatically influenced how we convey our product vision, strategy, and roadmap."

ALEX DEVE, DIRECTOR OF PRODUCT MANAGEMENT, FACEBOOK

"*Story 10x* delivers on a powerful premise: narrative intelligence is the future of leadership."

MONICA REED, FORMER CHIEF LEARNING OFFICER, ADVENTHEALTH

"An impressive read. In *Story 10x*, Michael Margolis shows how you can use narrative thinking (a gene hardwired in all of us) to create memorable, persuasive communications. As someone who needs to tell the story of innovation every day, I will be using the frameworks from this book to facilitate more powerful exchanges."

MAJA THOMAS, CHIEF INNOVATION OFFICER, HACHETTE LIVRE

"Story is the currency of culture. *Story 10x* makes a strong case for why the biggest innovations are a result of a great stories, as well as the framework to create your own."

ROBERT RICHMAN, FORMER PRODUCT MANAGER, ZAPPOS INSIGHTS

"Deep, disruptive, and refreshingly simple. This book will change the game for those leaders willing to lead with authenticity, ambition, and action."

SHANE CURREY, PARTNER, HUMAN CAPITAL, DESIGN FOR BUSINESS & NARRATIVE STRATEGY, DELOITTE AUSTRALIA

"Michael Margolis is a master storyteller. I initially reached out to him to help my design team to become better communicators, both in and outside of the company. He taught the team to tell a story, leading first with positive emotion and then backing up the claim with evidence— a brilliantly simple and effective sandwich method that I employ daily. *Story 10x* is a distillation of his years of experience and his deep-seated humanity, as he helps innovators to express their visions in language that is understandable by the C-suite. But perhaps, most importantly, his book teaches the reader about the value of telling an *Undeniable Story*—something we need in this day and age—the ability to describe a better future for us all. *Story 10x* inspires the notion that storytelling can save us as a species."

JOHN S. COUCH, VP, PRODUCT DESIGN, HULU

"Storytelling is the essence of all great experience design. In *Story 10x*, Michael will help you turn audiences into the heroes of their own journey."

BRIAN SOLIS, DIGITAL ANTHROPOLOGIST, FUTURIST, AND BESTSELLING AUTHOR OF *LIFESCALE*

"The most complicated part of innovation is not the idea; it's selling the idea. Read *Story 10x* if you want your ideas to see the light of day. It's not just another storytelling book. It's the most powerful sales tool you'll ever own."

STEPHEN SHAPIRO, AUTHOR OF *24/7 INNOVATION* AND *BEST PRACTICES ARE STUPID*

"Every new product launch, every political campaign, and every new venture shares the same strategic imperative: you must control the narrative. Finally, here's help from master storyteller Michael Margolis that tells you exactly how to do that by making your Story 10x better."

ROBERT TERCEK, AUTHOR OF *VAPORIZED* AND FORMER PRESIDENT, DIGITAL MEDIA, OWN: OPRAH WINFREY NETWORK

"Great leaders know the future is about transformation, not tweaks. Transformation requires an emotional connection only enabled by storytelling—and no one has lived in the trenches of strategic story-telling like Michael Margolis. You'll want to read *Story 10x*."

SAUL KAPLAN, FOUNDER AND CHIEF CATALYST, BUSINESS INNOVATION FACTORY

"Every day game-changing products and world-altering ideas fail. If you want to maximize the chances that yours will succeed, you'll need the one thing this book expertly teaches you how to create: a powerful story."

ROHIT BHARGAVA, BESTSELLING AUTHOR OF *NON-OBVIOUS* AND FOUNDER, THE NON-OBVIOUS COMPANY

"The great secret of growth—of any kind change, really—is that it all comes down to one factor: story. There's no better guide on the planet than Michael Margolis to help you employ story not only to your own advantage, but also to that of your company and our shared future. Whether you're trying to sell an idea to your senior leadership team, your kids, or your community, *Story 10x* is the blueprint for designing a narrative that can make your vision a reality."

SAM ROSEN, SENIOR VP, GROWTH, *THE ATLANTIC*

"The difference between a good marketer and a great one is their ability to tell the story. *Story 10x* offers the perfect bridge from good to great, unveiling the science behind storytelling. It offers tons of practical advice built on decades of helping marketing and product teams develop a mind for narrative. This book is a must-read for product marketers who are ready to own the story."

EVA WOO, GLOBAL VP, PRODUCT MARKETING, SAP SUCCESSFACTORS

"The most critical business skill for the next decade is storytelling. Period. Those who understand the power of narrative will succeed. *Story 10x* can be the tool that helps take your career (and your life) to the next level."

JOE PULIZZI, AUTHOR OF *CONTENT INC.*, *KILLING MARKETING*, AND *EPIC CONTENT MARKETING*

"Create opportunities through better storytelling. Love *Story 10x*."

KARE ANDERSON, TED SPEAKER WITH 2.4 MILLION VIEWS AND AUTHOR OF *MUTUALITY MATTERS*

"People love a good story. But how do you tell a story about something complex, technical, and occasionally boring? *Story 10x* is the answer, or at least 9x the answer."

DAVID NIHILL, AUTHOR OF *DO YOU TALK FUNNY?* AND FOUNDER, FUNNYBIZZ CONFERENCE

"*Story 10x* is the activating ingredient that will bring your world-changing idea to life."

PAMELA SLIM, AUTHOR OF *BODY OF WORK*

"*Story 10x* is a step-by-step guide on how to use data and narrative to stack the odds. Michael Margolis is the modern-day Joseph Campbell for business. This is the only book I have ever read that can teach you how to bend the curve of reality in your favor."

BLAKE EASTMAN, PROFESSIONAL POKER PLAYER AND FOUNDER, THE NONVERBAL GROUP

STORY 10X

TURN THE IMPOSSIBLE
INTO THE INEVITABLE

STORY 10X

MICHAEL MARGOLIS

STORIED

Cataloguing in publication information is available from Library and Archives Canada.

ISBN 978-1-989025-58-1 (hardcover)
ISBN 978-1-989025-59-8 (ebook)

Published by Storied
getstoried.com

Produced by Page Two
www.pagetwo.com

Jacket and interior design by Taysia Louie
Printed and bound in Canada by Friesens
Distributed in Canada by Raincoast Books
Distributed in the US and internationally by
Publishers Group West, a division of Ingram

19 20 21 22 23 5 4 3 2 1

getstoried.com
@getstoried
#story10x

Dedicated to the gods of story,
the creative source in all of us.

————————

Contents

"If you're going to have a story, have a big story, or none at all."

JOSEPH CAMPBELL

Introduction
The Power of Story 10X

THERE'S ONE STORY I never quite know how to tell.

Twenty years ago, I tried to make history. I cofounded a startup. I was a social entrepreneur: applying business principles to social change. Groundbreaking. Game-changing. Disruptive. It turned the world of nonprofits upside down. Not an ordinary startup.

Even in the late '90s, many of us had the sense that technology was going to change the world. And, within a blink of the eye, there was a talent gap with more than 500,000 tech jobs in the United States going unfilled. Our crazy idea? To build the training and development pathways for inner-city adults to get high-tech jobs. The organization was called CitySkills. Our focus was on bridging the digital divide.

This social venture was quickly embraced. *Fast Company* described our work as a "subtly subversive manifesto." Within a year, we were funded by the Ford and Rockefeller Foundations. I was advising the U.S. Department of Labor and a wide range of policymakers on this new workforce phenomenon and partnering with some of the leading tech companies and venture philanthropists of the day. There was no stopping me.

Within two years, it all came crashing down.

An epic startup failure by the age of 24.

CitySkills was an ambitious attempt at innovation. In many ways, it presaged the future. Twenty years later, our original mission is more relevant than ever. The digital divide still exists. As tech recruiting organization Andela describes it, "genius is equally distributed, but opportunity is not." And, as others in the field have said, the same huge questions remain: *Who gets to learn how to code, get a tech job, and build the companies of the future? What are the business and social incentives to equal the playing field? And what are the implications either way for the future of our culture and economy?*

Back in 2001, this story was ahead of its time. Admittedly, I probably wasn't the right front man. A nerdy, 20-something white Jewish boy, 30 pounds overweight. Yet, even then, I had an uncanny ability to frame and present big ideas. I knew how to capture people's imagination and invite people to dream a bigger dream. To me, this wasn't about saving the inner city. This was about discovering the skills that any of us need to thrive, much less survive, in the New Economy. Except I found myself up against deeply entrenched social norms, fears, and obstacles. It's not easy to talk about race, poverty, and human potential. Regardless of your age or appearance.

Riding the wave of the dot-com boom, my dreams eventually came crashing down. I discovered the riptide and heavy undertow created when worldviews and value systems collide. Especially when spreadsheets are running the asylum of social change. Something critical was missing from the conversation. It required a new way of thinking, a new vocabulary, a new way of seafaring.

I intuitively knew it. I just didn't have the language for it yet.

At the time, it was a riddle I couldn't solve. I felt misunderstood. Exhausted. And embarrassed. When CitySkills failed, my own health and ego suffered with it. I had given it everything I had, and I ended up seriously ill in the hospital. The first of many more physical struggles and trials to come.

It took me a couple years to regain my health, rebuild my life, and renew my professional path. While no one likes to fail, this experience served as an initiation and turning point. The inciting incident, in storytelling terms.

In retrospect, I'm lucky it came at such an early age.

This still didn't offer solace to all the unanswered questions that I had:

· How do you tell the story of disruptive innovation?
· Why do so many world-changing ideas get lost in translation?
· What makes social and cultural change so darn difficult?

Many of us wrestle with these fundamental questions. How to improve the human experience despite the odds. How to reimagine how business is done, regardless of established norms. How to defy the odds and create something totally new, different, and better.

In short, how to turn the impossible into the inevitable.

I knew I had to figure out how to tell this kind of story—the story of *innovation*.

This book is about that. And about my own surprising and unexpected journey. Developing messaging, pitches, and presentations for some of the most iconic leaders in the world. Twenty years of learning and experimentation. Working with hundreds of organizations and training tens of thousands. Testing my approach in the dojos of Silicon Valley, the conference rooms of Fortune 500s, and the town halls of local nonprofits. Creating narratives that sell billion-dollar, high-stakes initiatives. Humanizing tech products used by hundreds of millions of people every day. Helping reframe climate change, psychological testing, science education, supply chain transformation, public libraries, and the structure of belonging in the digital age.

There are always more big and important stories to tell. That's what makes this work so much fun.

I will share with you some of my insights and breakthroughs for your own disruptive storytelling and, more important, my hard-won lessons and failures in how to get your story straight. Please don't take my word for it. This book will help you explore this idea for yourself. The importance of storytelling has been recognized throughout human history. From kings and priests to memorable leaders. The ultimate act of power, influence, and culture creation.

BENDING THE CURVE OF REALITY IN YOUR FAVOR

At Amazon, Jeff Bezos has long implemented a unique meeting structure. Executives sit in silence, reading a six-page memo on the topic at hand. Bullet points are discouraged. The document must consist of a coherent narrative. After everyone has digested the "six-pager," the discussion begins and decisions are made.

Inside Facebook, every six months, product team leaders undergo the same ritual. They must create a written narrative about their work and present it to Mark Zuckerberg, Sheryl Sandberg, Chris Cox, and the rest of the executive team. Depending on how that vision, strategy, and roadmap is received, huge choices are made about the future of the product and about the trajectory of those leaders' careers.

Wall Street analysts and the media pay as much attention, if not more, to Warren Buffett's carefully written annual letter than they do the financials in the Berkshire Hathaway shareholder report. Buffett, long known for his principled approach to investing, loves telling the big-picture story about his portfolio companies and the general directions of the market. Buffett's principled storytelling is legendary, encouraging investors to hang on every word from the "Sage of Omaha."

Bezos, Zuckerberg, and Buffett. They're onto something. They know the story is *everything*.

True, these presentations are usually accompanied with lots of data. Yet *meaning* doesn't come from the numbers. Meaning comes from the story about what these numbers represent or tell us. The human brain is overwhelmed when confronted with abstract data. It seeks to find patterns and make connections. It needs context to put things into perspective. Emotional resonance establishes relevance. Only then do you need the evidence to validate and support your big ideas. Daniel Kahneman, Nobel Prize–winning economist and author of *Thinking, Fast and Slow*, underlines this need when he explains, "No one ever made a decision because of a number. They need a story."

Too often, we've been taught to believe that the data just speaks for itself. Sadly, it doesn't.

In business, we all face the same three constraints: (1) time, (2) money, and (3) people. Those are the forcing functions that shape and define our reality. *How can we go to market with just nine months of lead time?! We don't have the budget for that kind of build! We simply can't find enough qualified engineers to deliver against the product requirements.* And somehow we figure out how to make it work. Truth be told, we all wish we could bend reality in our favor. Well, with the right story, you can.

We all know charismatic leaders who sell billion-dollar dreams of a better tomorrow, to only see their pitches crash and fail under the light of scrutiny. As the ancient Greeks warned us in the story of Icarus, be careful about flying too close to the sun. Storytelling is no panacea, no cure-all. You have to actually deliver on the promise of what you're selling. To bring integrity to the process of speculation. In today's day and age, you have a shorter and shorter reputational runway. The transparency of technology means it's harder and harder to hide behind a lie. It eventually catches up to you. Just consider Elizabeth Holmes, founder and CEO of Theranos, who sold a $10 billion dream to build a revolutionary new science for testing blood. Despite modeling herself after Steve Jobs, down to the black turtleneck, it was a giant fraud. Same with Billy McFarland and the Fyre Festival, the world's greatest music festival that never was. In both cases, the dream was so powerful and alluring that audiences believed in the story despite the lack of evidence. At the end of the day, a story must deliver on its promise.

And yet bold, audacious dreams are turned into reality all the time. These are the times we live in. When you can build a true billion-dollar business in just three years. Or change the way the world thinks after posting a single viral video. In fact, you can stack the odds in your favor. When you align with the forces of storytelling and make the right offerings to the gods of innovation, something different happens. Magic happens. No obstacle is too big. No challenge is insurmountable. The perceived limitations of (1) time, (2) money, and (3) people can actually bend. Handled the right way, these limitations can stretch and defy the laws of gravity. Yes, this really happens. I've seen it happen countless times. Maybe you have too.

The secret? Knowing how to get your story straight.

When people are aligned in the same bigger story, you can move mountains.

That's what makes storytelling a *force multiplier*. 2x. 5x. Even 10x.

That's why this book is called *Story 10x*.

THE HEART OF THE STORYTELLER

Storytelling is much more than cute anecdotes or a once-upon-a-time fairy tales. At its heart, storytelling is about meaningfully communicating what we see, feel, and believe. An inspiring vision. The world we think is possible. The experiences we care about improving. And why it matters. Presented in such a compelling and attractive manner that we can't help but say *yes*.

The heart of the storyteller becomes the heart of the story. With the courage to have a point of view, to take a stand, to be bold and vulnerable. As my storytelling colleague Ameen Haque explains, "A story is a truth well told." Truth goes to the heart of trust, belief, and faith. And while this is not a book about religion, make no mistake: true transformational storytelling is sacred stuff. A secular form for the most essential meaningful matters of life.

You can't deliver on the promise of disruption without confronting the existential matters. That's what disruption really is. Redefining how we think and live—whether it's the food we eat, the way we travel, or how we approach family, relationships, finances, health, wellness, and so much more. Of course, disruption equally won't succeed without an effective business model, go-to-market strategy, and customer demand. You have to marry the big ideas with the fundamentally practical and sober aspects of life. The story of the future is up for grabs.

WHAT'S AHEAD: AN OVERVIEW OF THE BOOK

In this book, I'll teach you how to narrate the future. How to present your vision, strategy, and approach in *undeniable* terms. Understand the proper use of data. What you must do to set the table and create a receptive field for your ideas. This is a fateful choice. I've seen careers made and broken in these defining moments. Whether you're trying to get executive sponsorship for your big idea or pitching investors for your next round of capital. Whether you're standing in front of thousands at a company all-hands or you're trying to align teams and cross-functional counterparts. Too often, we face competing narratives. Alternative versions of the story—shaped by conflicting worldviews, value systems, agendas, interests, or just a flat-out difference of opinion.

Communicating ideas is not a lost cause. You just have to find and craft a story we can all agree on. That reminds us of what we share in common and transcends where we stand apart.

The key to creating an *Undeniable Story*, a story your audience cannot resist, is to learn how to *think in narrative*. A narrative mindset is at the heart of all successful innovation and transformation. This crucial way of thinking is an essential skill for leaders in a rapidly changing world. If you know how to change the story, you can change *anything*.

In Part I, you will learn about *narrative mindset*. I'll introduce you to some of my favorite insights from the fields of cultural anthropology, neuroscience, and comparative religion to explain how storytelling has historically shaped the human species. More important, we'll explore how storytelling is changing in today's rapidly evolving culture and the context of disruption. We'll also look at the mythic aspects of being a change agent and address a defining paradox. It often takes an outsider to create something disruptive, yet culture is both sanctioned and sustained by the insiders. Resolving this tension is a critical part of the success of any innovator going forward. It's the only way you can deliver on the promise of a better future. This is where your own personal story is inextricably linked to the bigger story. Learning how to weave these together is both an art and science.

In Part II, we'll shift to *narrative methodology*. I'll present a three-step Storytelling Method for how to craft your own *Undeniable Story*. I'll show you how to use it in any high-stakes presentation where you need to sell the future and defend the past. These are the same principles and playbook that I've taught to senior executives at hundreds of iconic organizations around the world. That have been applied to projects where billions of dollars hang in balance. That have shaped advising high-stakes initiatives from private equity pitch decks to Fortune 100 innovation labs. I will introduce you to how you can build storytelling as an organizational capability for product, design, marketing, sales, or engineering teams. You'll learn the key ingredients to craft a breakthrough narrative. And you'll become more aware of the potential pitfalls—the "exits out of the story"—where your audience may feel judged, challenged, or rejected by your disruptive message. Our goal is to reduce or remove the *exits*. That's anywhere you're encouraging your audience to be on the defensive and to opt out. The right story in the right context can literally change the world. You just need to create a receptive field that reframes your radical ideas into a reasonable leap.

This book is built to handle the biggest, most complex stories of our time. The future of tech, finance, healthcare, education, the environment, social progress, democracy, and so much more. Whether you're transforming an entire field or industry, tackling large systemic change, or exploring new ground at the grassroots level, this book will help you shape the breakthrough narrative. One that holds up to the complexities and challenges of business and cultural transformation.

BUILD A BIGGER FUTURE
WITH BETTER STORYTELLING

During the two decades since my first startup fail, I've been testing and refining how to tell the story of disruptive innovation. In the process, I've trained 60,000 leaders in hundreds of major organizations around the world. Across four continents, 16 countries, 34 industries—and innumerable cultures. The fundamental principles remain the same. I'm excited to share with you the fruits of my journey.

It's my dream that, 20 years from now, *narrative intelligence* will be the foundation of business leadership. A discipline taught in every business school, corporate university, and leadership accelerator around the world. I dream that the ideas presented in this book become best practices in the leadership curricula of tomorrow. Next-level leadership is narrative intelligence. Which is why I'm excited to share with you everything in this book.

This book introduces a storytelling school of thought built for a new age of communications. Unlocking its power is in the nuances. First, you have to get personal, as authentic connection and point of view are increasingly the currencies of our time. Second, it requires faith in the future, a belief in forward progress, no matter the evolutionary constraints. And lastly, it requires curiosity and humility, as storytelling is nothing less than an examination of the human experience. To become a master storyteller is to master life itself. This is an endless process. Especially in disruptive times. The best stories are the ones that inspire possibility and unleash human potential.

It's time we all learn this new kind of story.

The future depends on it.

"Great stories happen to those who can tell them."

———

IRA GLASS

PART I

THINKING IN NARRATIVE

"Any sufficiently advanced technology is indistinguishable from magic."

———

ARTHUR C. CLARKE

1

Storytelling in the Age of Disruption

IN THIS CHAPTER

- **Storytelling is powerful magic**

- **How to make the future irresistible**

- **Disruption and resistance**

- **The difference between story and narrative**

- **Applying the new language of disruption**

LIKE A LOT of kids, I was fascinated by magic.

In one of my earliest memories, my brother, David, and I put on a magic show in our living room for a big group of friends. We took our show very seriously. With our black capes and magic wands, we looked the part. Most important, however, we had something very special. The one thing that every great magician has in their vocabulary: a magic word.

And not just any magic word. We had the magic word guaranteed to turn the ordinary into the miraculous: *Abracadabra.*

It's a common but remarkably potent word. With historical origins lost in the mists of time. Some believe the word comes from the ancient Aramaic phrase "avra kehdabra": "I will create as I speak."

In a nutshell, that is the magic of words. They create.

Words, ideas, dreams, and even entire universes.

In the same way my brother's palm was empty one second and held a foam egg the next, words can conjure up something that didn't exist before.

We use the word "magic" to describe the indescribable. That which defies expectations.

Why all this talk about magic?

Because we live in extraordinary times. When there is a shorter half-life between ideas and reality than ever before. Imagine if,

"Innovation—any new idea—by definition will not be accepted at first. It takes repeated attempts, endless demonstrations, monotonous rehearsals before innovation can be accepted and internalized by an organization. This requires courageous patience."

WARREN BENNIS

a few hundred years ago, I told you that one day you would fly through the sky in a large metal tube, covering thousands of miles in just a matter of hours. At a time when traveling such distances took months. Sometimes years. Or that you could call up the world's knowledge at your fingertips, by simply stating out loud, "Siri, what are the lyrics to Beyoncé's 'Crazy in Love'?" You would have called me downright mad and possessed. Though you might appreciate my discerning taste in music.

The words we use really do make the world.

Every great leader is both a storyteller and a magician. The very best leaders are well versed in the art and science of story. They make magical things happen with their words. "The real secret of magic is that the world is made of words, and that if you know the words that the world is made of, you can make of it whatever you wish," said cultural futurist Terence McKenna.

In short, language is reality.

So, how do you weave magic into your big narrative? How do you help people see a new view when it involves disruptive ideas that challenge assumptions and expectations?

THE 90 PERCENT TEST

Take a moment and think of an audience you need to win over.

Your CEO. The board of directors. A prospective customer. A potential lead investor. A challenging stakeholder who holds your fate in their hands.

You're about to face this audience. And the stakes are high. Imagine them in your mind's eye. What do you see? How do you feel? Are you confident in the story you're about to share?

Business is filled with these defining moments. Moments that make the difference between success and failure, collaboration or opposition. Defining moments are shaped by what is said, how it is said, and how it lands with your audience. What will truly inspire and influence?

Now imagine yourself again in front of that audience. Your heart is beating fast, sweat is beginning to bead, and your mouth is running dry. It's a high-stakes interaction with your vision, funding, message, product, or cause on the line. The future hangs in the balance.

You think you've got 15 minutes—or perhaps half an hour—to persuade your audience and get them on your side.

In reality, you only have five minutes to get 90 percent of the room on your side.

The 90 percent test is a great gut-check exercise. I was originally introduced to the premise by Antony Brydon, CEO of Directly, during one of our pitch development sessions. What you say or do in those first few minutes determines everything that follows. If you can't inspire your audience, make them curious, and capture their imagination, chances are you never will.

What can you say or do in those precious first five minutes?

What will you share to get them on your side?

You have two choices—the Sledgehammer or the Ice Cream Cone.

Door #1: Sledgehammer

Walk in with a sledgehammer, challenge
assumptions, and forcefully shift their paradigm.

Door #2: Ice Cream Cone

Walk in with an ice cream cone, make people
feel good, and create a momentum of yes.

Which door do you choose?

Spending much of my time in Silicon Valley, working closely with brilliant executives who are disrupting industries and building the future, I have to confess that I see Door #1 chosen far more often than Door #2. And with good reason.

If you choose Door #1, you're sure to get a rise out of your audience. Perhaps even a mic-drop moment. But good luck getting everyone on your side. You'll leave many of them suspicious, defensive, and resistant to your message. While a sledgehammer is a dramatic, symbolic tool preferred by rebels (cue: Apple's iconic 1984 commercial), it leads to a lot of suffering and broken glass.

If you choose Door #2, you're going to put a smile on their face. Who doesn't like ice cream? Feeling good is contagious. You're more likely to pique curiosity, leaving them intrigued and hungry for more. Yes begets more yes. They'll see you as an ally around shared interests or needs, and they'll be open to your message rather than closed to it.

As an innovator and change agent, you're programmed to confront and challenge the status quo. To show people how things are wrong, bad, or broken. And what is required to fix it. While you may have truth on your side, who likes to be told they are wrong, bad, or stupid? In fairness, this is just conditioned behavior. We all want to be right. Yet, when you learn to tell your story in a manner that goes beyond right/wrong, you can truly move the needle, bend the curve, and transform your world.

Will you pass the 90 percent test? Will most people say yes and embrace what you have to say? Or will they say no and reject it?

These are defining moments for your business—and for you— and this book is all about teaching you how to get the most out of them.

WHY IS STORYTELLING SO HARD?

If you're reading this book, you're probably working on a big vision, a breakthrough product, a world-changing technology. You're leading a business transformation. Developing a new product that challenges the status quo. Changing the way your industry operates. Doing something that's never been done before. You know that what you're doing matters. You can feel it in your heart, mind, and gut. It's important, with many people's lives on the line. Except it's so big and complex you're not always sure how to talk about it. And people don't always respond like you wish they would.

If storytelling is such an elemental aspect of humanity, why do so many of us think we suck at it?

That core question haunted me for years. In fairness, the stories that we as innovators and change agents are trying to share are exceedingly hard to tell. Difficult to understand. When telling the story of disruption and innovation, traditional methods of storytelling just don't cut it. Because classical storytelling is a morality tale. Who's right? Who's wrong? We'll explore this storytelling structure more in Chapter 3, as well as the effects that different stories have on your brain and biology. In simple terms, disruption generates a defensive immune response. When people's fundamental beliefs are challenged, they reflexively go into a state of resistance. It's self-preservation at work.

Ambitious change and transformation are hard to see, imagine, or fathom. Especially when it's never been done before. Disruptive technologies are redefining the very notions of reality. How we date and find a life partner. How we invest money and plan for the future. How we order tacos at two in the morning. If your job is to sell the potential of a disruptive technology, then you have to reimagine and explain how a new surface, interaction points, formats, or customer experience journey will have a dramatic impact on user needs. You're trying to tell a story about the future to an audience that can't imagine or see what you're talking about. No wonder you feel lost in translation.

Disruption is not an easy or obvious story to tell. In the act of disruption, you're by definition doing something you're not "supposed" to do. You are challenging existing standards. Overstepping what was previously thought as acceptable or possible. As we'll explore in later chapters, it's hard for most audiences to accept this. Few people simply say, *Oh, right, thanks!* when you suggest to them that their world and beliefs just might be flawed.

And yet we continue to try to convince others in this very way.

"It ought to be remembered
that there is nothing more difficult
to take in hand, more perilous to
conduct, or more uncertain in its
success, than to take the lead in
the introduction of a new order of
things. Because the innovator
has for enemies all those who have
done well under the old conditions,
and lukewarm defenders in those who
may do well under the new."

———————

NICCOLÒ MACHIAVELLI

HOW TO MAKE THE FUTURE IRRESISTIBLE

To tell a disruptive story, you need a new approach.

You need a new kind of story.

What I call Story 10x. This book is all about teaching you how to craft an *Undeniable Story*.

Story 10x presents your big disruptive idea—in a manner that is difficult if not impossible to reject. Reframing the impossible into the inevitable.

It consists of three critical steps, described in the second part of this book.

STORY	NARRATIVE	STORY > NARRATIVE
Set-up	Context	Present the future in aspirational terms—how change leads to opportunity
Conflict	Emotion	Build empathy, describing the gap between desire and dilemma
Resolution	Evidence	Provide supporting data that legitimizes the promise of your big idea

An *Undeniable Story* is vastly more captivating than an anecdote and far more inspiring than "make believe." An *Undeniable Story* is a strategic narrative that transports your audience into the future—leading them on a journey beyond the world they know to the promised land of possibility. It conveys a new vision, strategy, and roadmap so convincingly and compellingly that your audience can't help but see it, feel it, and believe it. In short, they want what you're selling. Because your idea is a self-evident truth that people can relate to.

"Everything that can be invented has been invented."
CHARLES H. DUELL, COMMISSIONER, U.S. OFFICE OF PATENTS, 1899

"I think there is a world market for maybe five computers."
THOMAS WATSON, CHAIRMAN OF IBM, 1943

"This 'telephone' has too many shortcomings to be seriously considered as a means of communication. The device is inherently of no value to us."
WESTERN UNION INTERNAL MEMO, 1876

"Who the hell wants to hear actors talk?"
H.M. WARNER, COFOUNDER, WARNER BROTHERS, 1927

"We don't like their sound, and guitar music is on the way out."
DECCA RECORDS REJECTING THE BEATLES, 1962

"Louis Pasteur's theory of germs is ridiculous fiction."
PIERRE PACHET, PROFESSOR OF PHYSIOLOGY AT TOULOUSE, 1872

"Heavier-than-air flying machines are impossible."
LORD KELVIN, PRESIDENT, ROYAL SOCIETY, 1895

"640K ought to be enough for anybody."
BILL GATES, CEO, MICROSOFT, 1981

In Part I of *Story 10x*, I'll help you understand why we need a narrative structure like this when trying to present and sell disruptive innovation. And in Part II of the book, I'll walk you through each of these three steps in explicit detail with lots of working examples and nuanced distinctions.

When effectively crafted, an *Undeniable Story* has the power to 10x your future.

In Silicon Valley, a place that reveres exponential thinking, teams are encouraged to solve at a 10x level. In most organizations, 10 percent growth is considered a respectable outcome or improvement. Yet it's incremental innovation. In contrast, 10x growth represents disruptive innovation, impact at a next-level order of magnitude. When you're talking about making disruptive change, aim for 10x growth.

An *Undeniable Story* can do all that, and more.

DISRUPTION AND RESISTANCE

Business is built on persuasion, and persuasion is rooted in story.

If you're like most innovators, you see the world as it could be. You believe beyond a shadow of a doubt in your idea. You know it has the potential to change the game. To unlock value creation. To make things better. To transform the user experience. And deliver oversized results. It's just that not everyone sees it as you do. In fact, you're going to come across lots of people who don't understand, care, or trust in what you're saying.

Fact: most people aren't easily persuaded when presented with a disruptive idea. Especially when it calls into question our existing worldview. Our natural human reaction is to become skeptical, suspicious, even defensive. Because in all likelihood, your New

Story directly challenges the validity of the Old Story. So, we're likely going to feel judged as wrong, bad, or stupid.

That's what happens when you challenge the status quo.

Innovation and transformation are by definition acts of defiance. For most of us, they trigger a fear response. Resistance is the enemy of the new. It can kill a bold, new initiative before it ever sees the day of light. It has the power to stunt the potential of even the greatest world-changing breakthrough, the most visionary business transformation, and the freshest radical solution.

Disruption is eating the world. For every new innovation, you'll find a competing story trying to stem the flood. Airbnb has upended the monopoly of the hospitality industry. Municipalities are pushing back, as Airbnb disrupts real estate rental markets and affordable housing. Yet Airbnb also has led to great new opportunities. Many homeowners credit Airbnb for helping them generate a second income that they need to survive or get ahead. And many travelers love Airbnb as a way to get to know the real soul of a place and live like a local, even if for just a rare, magic moment. The point is disruption is a multifaceted story. And you'll always face a range of alternative stories that argue the teller's interpretation of reality. Which means you better have a strong *Undeniable Story* to overcome the competing currents.

Changing the narrative is a heretical act. But it's also one of the most powerful ways to transform culture. Whether inside a company, country, or community. Ten years ago, who would have thought that today we would be debating whether we want self-driving cars in our community? Or if we should entertain the idea of booking a flight to space with Richard Branson's Virgin Galactic startup? Or if robots have their electronic eyes on our jobs? Heresy.

The narrative has changed, fundamentally and forever. The magic show has begun.

In this book, you'll learn more about why the stories of transformational change—the stories you are trying to tell the world—are heretical. You'll discover how these stories make your audience feel. You'll find out who these heretics are (hint: they are all around you—in fact, they probably *are* you). You'll glimpse the magic of turning the heretical into the undeniable. And you'll see why storytelling may be the most advanced yet basic technology we have at our disposal today.

We celebrate and honor the visionaries. Those who dare to dream a bigger dream. And those among us who challenge the status quo and redefine what is possible. Along the way, it's worth remembering there was a time when magic was considered heresy too. History has always been shaped, defined, and refined by the heretics. The game changers. The disruptors. But you don't have to die for your cause. There's a different and better way forward.

WHAT CAN AN *UNDENIABLE* STORY DO FOR YOU?

When you learn this new way of narrative, you have the magical power to inspire and influence in ways you've only ever dreamed of. This is why *Forbes* calls storytelling "the #1 most important career skill for the future." Yet until now, few books or resources have tackled the application of storytelling to communicate the new and build the future.

As we've seen, disruption is a difficult story to tell.

If you're a C-level executive, you need a corporate narrative that conveys your vision, strategy, and roadmap. In other words—who we are, where we are going, and how we are going to get there. This narrative is critical to how you lead your company. It's hard to inspire people with OKRs (objectives and key results) alone—such as, in the case of one of our clients: revenue of $2 billion, subscriber base of 25 million, and a net promoter score of 50. Not exactly soul-stirring material for thousands of employees. OKRs are an incredible tool! They just need to be combined with a compelling vision that inspires people to want to climb the summit and overcome the obstacles along the way.

When you shift your strategy, you have to shift your story.

People want to be part of a bigger story. Unfortunately, most companies move so fast that it's easy for your people to get lost—to no longer know what story they are in. You have to take the time to bring everybody along. I frequently see gaps between the narratives at the executive, manager, and individual contributor levels. As a leader, it's your responsibility to present and deliver a next-level narrative that unites everyone. A way for it to resonate with investors, employees, customers, new hires, and anyone who is a critical stakeholder to your future.

If you're VP of a business unit or functional discipline, you need a narrative that conveys the value of your work. You always need to sell up to senior management, to get sponsorship for next year's budget, head count, and priorities. You also have to work well with your cross-functional counterparts who sometimes have competing needs and interests. You forever have to juggle the demands of the core business with where you'd like to be innovating. A big enough story allows you to access more (1) time, (2) money, and (3) people to achieve your goals.

If you're a manager, odds are you're easily caught in the weeds of execution. You're not far removed from the frontline delivery. Perhaps you've recently been promoted to a manager position. Here's some news: what got you to where you are now won't get you to where you need to go next. As a manager, your success comes down to managing *people*, not just delivering on the actual work. That means your soft skills—including empathy, trust, and communication—are what make the real difference. You're used to being evaluated on the quality of your work, how you meet OKRs, and the metrics to support your progress. Except the data, the product, the design never speaks for itself. You need to learn how to build a business case, speak to a bigger set of ideas and opportunities, and ensure you don't get co-opted by cross-functional counterparts.

While we're at it, let's take a moment to look at some of the key functional disciplines of the modern organization.

If you're a head of product, it's your task to contextualize how your products are impacting the lives of your customer/user/member. You have to translate a product roadmap filled with technical features and functions into a big-picture story that can inspire and influence.

If you're a head of design, you must represent the voice of the user and teach the rest of your company how to design more human-centric experiences. You also have to advocate for the role of design as a lynchpin of business transformation. This isn't about design as pretty pixels or frosting on the cake. But rather about the existential soul of what your product, service, or solutions do in people's lives—and how it feels when they interact with your brand experience.

If you're a head of marketing, you're being asked to communicate with customers in a whole new way. To humanize what are often highly technical and complex products. And deliver a tone that is more interactive, transparent, and participatory—where customers have a voice in the brand story and community.

Same is true with heads of sales, where you must take a more consultative approach with your prospective buyers, who are weary of one-size-fits-all solutions and frankly hate the feeling of "being sold to." Every customer seems themselves as a "unique snowflake" with distinct needs and preferences. They require a

21 Ways an *Undeniable Story* Can Make a Difference

You want to tell the right story for the future you want to create. When you learn the three basic steps to an *Undeniable Story*, you can use them to achieve a wide range of desired outcomes. What gets you to advance from contributor to manager to leader is not your functional excellence. It's your ability to master communications. The best leaders are the best storytellers. When you craft an *Undeniable Story*, you can . . .

1   Create a strategic narrative that brings everyone together
2   Get executive buy-in for your vision, strategy, and roadmap
3   Secure capital from investors and/or next-level sponsorship
4   Clarify the business case and value of what you do
5   Convey the potential of a disruptive technology
6   Successfully deliver on the promise of transformation
7   Create alignment across cross-functional teams
8   Translate a product roadmap into a big-picture story
9   Legitimize your work and progress in a quarterly business review
10 Overcome obstacles and resistance to change
11 Turn data into insights that influence decision-making
12 Shift perceptions on a complex and divisive issue
13 Recruit the hard-to-hire talent that can accelerate your business
14 Turn your ideas into thought leadership that shapes the conversation
15 Create a sense of belonging that leads to high-performance culture
16 Demonstrate empathy and care for the people you serve
17 Develop the executive presence needed to navigate in uncertain times
18 Unite diverse stakeholders around shared common interests
19 Influence even when you don't have the formal authority
20 Advance your career on senior management track
21 Turn the impossible into the inevitable

new way of breaking through with sales conversations that deepen rapport, trust, and relationships.

Lastly, if you're leading human resources or learning and development, you're tasked with the Herculean feat of retooling talent to lead in the 21st century. You have to recruit and onboard thousands of new employees to embrace and belong in a fast-moving business culture.

At every level, storytelling gets to the heart of the matter.

STORY VS. NARRATIVE

Before we go further, let's consider the difference between story and narrative. This one distinction is the basis of Narrative Strategy, an emerging discourse increasingly embraced in Silicon Valley and by anyone who needs to sell a disruptive future.

Here's why. Story, in its simplest form, is about a character and the things that happen to them. As author Michael Lewis defines it, "A story is—people and situations."

A story has a beginning, middle, and end. Through which we explore the desire, dilemmas, and choices that a character faces. Think of a story as an anecdote or vignette that recounts specific moments, with a time and place. It provides us with entertainment, insight, or even a life lesson. It creates a shared emotional experience that can bond us together. A customer story. A product story. A "values in action" story. A new employee onboarding story.

Therein lies the challenge—in business, we are swimming in a sea of stories. *Everyone* has a story. From the boardroom to the employees to social media. Infinite stories. Billions and trillions of stories. And every story matters.

In such an environment, how can you make sense and meaning of things, much less get everyone aligned around a shared story?

That's the role and the power of narrative. Defining the frame.

In contrast to story, a narrative is much bigger. It's a way of looking at the world. An overarching concept that influences sense-making and decision-making. It doesn't necessarily have a clear beginning, middle, and end like a story does. A narrative most often unfolds over a period of time. Which means the conclusion is still up for grabs!

Whether complex or simple, there are always competing narratives.

A narrative at its most basic level can be a contrasting point of view. For example, the catchy Miller Lite campaign "tastes great" versus "less filling" pits two perspectives of fandom playfully against each other. A more complex narrative like the American Dream is a touchstone that has inspired countless generations. It embodies the belief that no matter who you are or where you come from, in America you can create a better future. There are many stories that illustrate this narrative from the real life of Oprah to the fictional legend of the Great Gatsby. Even today, there is a great political debate around the American Dream, and who can access it. If each story is like a pearl, then a narrative is the necklace.

Pearls strung together to form a larger, interconnected meaning. Narrative connects the dots at the big-picture level, using a range of stories to illustrate, animate, and validate its message. Narrative gives meaning to a broader vision, shows what's possible, and tells us why we should head in that direction.

To bring the future to life, you need a narrative. A story usually describes the past, a point in time. The future is more speculative—filled with a range of possibilities. True, you can write science fiction about the future. But it's called science *fiction*. With a much greater risk of overshooting expectations and believability. There is a whole field devoted to scenario planning or future forecast work: an exercise in long-term view, with research on the deep future trends that will remake the world. We work with UX research teams all the time who have to translate their insights into a business case and find a product owner to commercialize their insights. But for most of you, this kind of storytelling is too far afield.

The majority of the time, clients need a narrative for existing opportunities. How they are going to deliver against ambitious goals and expectations over the next 12 to 24 months. On a project with one of the largest social networks in the world, we worked on the future of community-building for a product team that has hundreds of millions of "power users." In that case, exactly how many stories are there? Millions! That's why an overarching narrative was so critical to being able to present to and influence executive management. That narrative about the structure of belonging in the digital age—and how people's sense of identity, relationships, and connection is changing—had an oversized impact across the entire company and a dozen other products in its vast ecosystem.

If you try to communicate at such an epic and high-stakes level without a clear distinction between story and narrative, your message is likely to get lost in translation. Or fall apart under the weight of its apparent complexity to skeptical audiences. In the face of complexity, disruption, and business transformation, what organizations need is a bigger story. Especially in defining moments such as quarterly business reviews, all-hands meetings, and investor pitches.

Hopefully, you're starting to see how narrative is crucial for anybody trying to shift the status quo. It's what helps people see the forest from the trees. To make strategic sense and meaning. And align the trajectory forward. Few companies give their leaders a structure or model for this. To communicate the breakthrough work being done by you or your team, a simple closed-loop story does not go deep enough to portray a disruptive vision, product, or idea. You need to go further.

You need to think in narrative.

That's what an *Undeniable Story* is all about. It's an approach to storytelling that's worked for hundreds of organizations around the world, from Fortune 500s to early stage startups. It gives you the tools and the language to think in narrative, no matter what the circumstance. No matter the industry, field, or sector. Because once you can think in narrative, you can reframe the narrative. And that's the key to making any disruptive story stick the landing.

So, I have a favor to ask you. Now that we've looked at the distinction between a story and a narrative, for simplicity's sake, I'll ask that you set it aside until we return to it in Chapter 7. In this book, I often use story or storytelling as the default term, since it's the turn of phrase we are most familiar with. Yet remember this: even though storytelling is the label we recognize and use, *narrative* is what brings us the most valuable prize.

STORY	NARRATIVE	STORY > NARRATIVE
Set-up	Context	Setting: set scene/what's changing
Conflict	Emotion	Character: complex desire/dilemma
Resolution	Evidence	Proof: that this is real/possible

THE NEW STORYTELLING: A LANGUAGE FOR DISRUPTION

Since the first cave and rock paintings 50,000 years ago, storytelling has kept evolving to reflect changes in culture and context. This is why we need a new storytelling best suited for 21st-century transformation. From papyrus to television, each new story technology required its own syntax and structure. A language tailor-made to the medium and its corresponding era.

Each new language first had to dislodge an old one. It took years, for example, for filmmakers to create movies that used the true language of film rather than the borrowed language of theater—in terms of scenes, dialogue, and more. They eventually learned how to use camera positions and angles, lighting, color, shot sizes, movement, sound, and editing to tell a story uniquely appropriate for the medium of film. We're in the midst of the same evolution today, as social media transforms the context and syntax of how people tell their stories. It's also completely upended the traditional control and approach of business institutions by demanding new levels of transparency, emotionality, and collaboration in our storytelling.

When you have a transformational story to share, you need to do so much more than tell a great anecdote. You have to frame the bigger picture, the opportunity at hand. You have to narrate the emotional content and validate people's feelings. You have to help your audience believe in how this vision is achievable and why they can (and should) trust you to deliver on it.

If your message challenges the status quo, upends norms, or announces a radical breakthrough, it is time to put aside the traditional language of storytelling. Why? Because it is simply not as effective in this era of rapid transformation as it was in the past.

It's time to learn the new language of disruption and to create stories that use it.

This book draws on dozens of examples from almost 20 years working across Silicon Valley, Fortune 500, and global changemaking organizations. I'll go over a wide range of use case examples drawn from the trenches. Where an *Undeniable Story*, and the language of disruption, made all the difference. For example...

- How to sell a vision for the future of work and a new $2 billion corporate campus

- How to pitch VCs on a Series B investment for a sustainable apparel pioneer

- How a head of product reframes community-building for 100 million power users

- How the design lab of a major corporation is redefining the future of retail

- How environmentalists can develop positive, inspiring campaigns for climate change

- How research scientists try to provide internet access to every person on the planet

- How to save a $20 million science education program on the congressional chopping block

- How a large membership organization can rewrite the narrative on aging

- How a coalition frames the role and value of public libraries in the digital age

- How a VP of design leads transformation, reimagining the UX for 25 million subscribers

Story 10x is a new discourse for the age of disruption. In the chapters to come, you will learn the science and psychology behind this new story philosophy. You will see examples of how and why an *Undeniable Story* works. You will learn the keys to unlock it.

By the end, you will be able to tell your own *Undeniable Story*. One that has the power to change the world.

THE HOLY GRAIL OF STORY

Let's recap.

As a driver of innovation, you know that your success depends directly on how readily people embrace your ideas. Yet stories of disruption are among the hardest to tell. Innovation is intrinsically heretical. It threatens the status quo and demands your audience to believe in an unknown future. It's often too big a leap for people to make. Innovation naturally triggers fear and resistance.

In this age of disruption, much of what we've been taught about business presentations and storytelling is obsolete. If you point to old problems and promise to save the world from them, you're telling your audience that the old way—the way they know and are comfortable with—is wrong, bad, or stupid. This puts them on the defensive. You can have the most game-changing story in the world, and their ears and hearts will be closed to it.

What you need is a story that captures people from the get-go, that cuts through their resistance, that shows them why your vision matters and why they should care. You need a story that gets 90 percent of the people in the room on your side in the first five minutes, without triggering their fear.

An anecdote likely won't do that. Unless you're an absolute master storyteller.

In contrast, an *Undeniable Story* can. No matter how bad of a public speaker or performer you are, you can inspire and influence others with your *Undeniable Story*. It's all based on your ability to think in narrative and to present complex situations in a simple yet compelling manner. This will transform how you structure and communicate any disruptive idea for greater impact.

One thing is as true in the age of disruption as it has ever been. To tell a persuasive story, you have to know your audience. They are the reason your story exists. To craft an *Undeniable Story*, you must focus on who your audience is and shape your story around them. You'll learn how to do that in Part II of this book.

As important as they are, your audience is only *half* the reason your story exists. The other half is *you*. A story is about the intimate relationships built between the teller and the listener. Who exactly are you asking your audience to connect with? And how can they trust and relate to you? That's what we'll explore in the next chapter.

"All great literature is
one of two stories;
a man goes on a
journey or a stranger
comes to town."

———

JOHN GARDNER

2

From Outsider
to Insider

IN THIS CHAPTER

- **Making your message personal**

- **The outsider as a cultural hero**

- **How to be right without making others wrong**

- **Why you need to tell your personal story**

- **What to do with your story once you have it**

WHEN I WAS nine years old, my family moved to an exotic and foreign land.

Los Angeles, California.

Although I was born in the United States, at the age of three months, we relocated to Switzerland. In a small idyllic town outside Lausanne, we were the only American family in a bedroom community of 5,000. I attended a French-language public school and spent my childhood assimilating into the francophone culture of this postcard-picture little corner of Europe.

Then, one evening, in the fall of 1985, my parents sat my brother and me down at the dinner table. They had surprising news. In just a few months, we would be moving back to the United States.

After spending almost the entire first nine years of my life in Switzerland, I considered myself to be more Swiss than American. Even if I was a bit strange and different to the locals. What little I knew of the land of my birth was mostly the result of annual trips to visit family during the holidays. New York. South Florida. Chicago. Those were the places I was familiar with. Aside from what I saw in American films and television shows, Los Angeles was unknown territory.

As my parents spoke, I wondered about the new life that awaited us.

I was extremely anxious about this change, but there was nothing I could do about it. What would happen to the friends I left behind? Would they forget about me? Would I make new friends in the United States? America was my place of origin, but I was an outsider there. I would soon find out I wasn't American enough. But I was equally never Swiss enough. I would forever be seen as an outsider. I was caught between two countries, two cultures, two worlds.

Language was one daunting hurdle I had to deal with as soon as I arrived. Though I had regularly spoken English at home with my parents, French was my first language. I hadn't bothered to learn to write in English—there was no need to. That would soon change.

I was then (and still am) a nerd. As a chubby and awkward kid, I couldn't play American sports (football, baseball, or basketball) to save my life. Any sports, for that matter. God knows I tried. I remember my dread and anxiety every day at recess in elementary school. I'd quietly and nervously stand in anguish, waiting to be picked for whatever team sport we were playing. A good day was simply being picked second to last.

Making the shift from a Swiss lederhosen boy to a California surfer-skater kid didn't make for a feel-good story. I was bullied every day. Life was a giant pile of suck.

During those years, creativity became my refuge. A place of comfort and safety where I could be myself and not feel pressure to fit in. Cheered on by our dad, a mad scientist, and our mom, a teacher/artist/toy designer, my brother and I built art installations and did science experiments. "Our home is an EXPLORATORIUM" was the first line in our family motto. (Really.)

My mother taught us to go to garage sales and pick out the best possible "superjunk." What others considered trash was our treasure: faded *Life* magazines from the 1950s. Antique cars, trucks, and other toys. And infinite boxes of every shape and size. We would assemble these materials into an imaginary world in honor

Margolis Family Motto (written by my mom, Leslie)

Our home is an EXPLORATORIUM.
There are no rules on what or how to create.
There is no one saying *you can't do that*...
It's too crazy or *we already tried that before.*
There is only imagination,
the everyday materials of life,
and our willingness to explore them.

of a subject, person, or theme. I didn't realize it then, but this was one of my first and most profound lessons in storytelling. Building a world in a box.

In retrospect, the family I grew up in created the perfect environment to cultivate a brain on story. Or at least one half of the story: the creative spark. The other half, the ability to find my tribe and community, was a bigger struggle. That's because, over time, my identity came to depend on being "different." I was not like the others, and I saw no obvious way to overcome my sense of separation and loneliness. It would take me decades to unpack this abiding sense of being an outsider. That I didn't fit in or belong.

According to developmental psychologists, every one of us has a defining moment, somewhere around the age of 9 to 11, that underpins the arc or theme of our lives.

What's your most vivid memory from that time in your life?

Chances are it involves a huge shock or disappointment, a moment that painfully challenged how you believed the world works. Most of us spend the rest of our lives trying to reconcile that disconnect. We also often find our professional passion, purpose, and inspiration from these early life experiences. Odds are there are stories from your own childhood and early career that you can use to help convey your vision and motivations as a leader.

Notice that we know the backstories of the most inspiring icons and leaders of the world. How Bill Gates dropped out of Harvard to start Microsoft, and that he's an absolute genius despite his sometimes-awkward social habits. Or that Oprah overcame trauma and abuse as a child, and perhaps even developed her depth of empathy and compassion out of her own suffering. Making sense of your own personal backstory and struggle is the first step in learning how to think in narrative. Your own life story is what is closest to you. It's what you've lived; it's in your bones; it's yours to tell.

It will be critical in establishing a personal connection with your audience. Before you can craft an *Undeniable Story* for the work you do, you need to take stock of your personal arc, vulnerabilities, and strengths—especially the ones that can become blind spots (more on that soon). It's only when you find your voice, identity, and confidence as an individual—and that includes coming to terms with your own journey as an outsider—that you can meaningfully connect with your tribe or audience and become the leader everyone is waiting for you to be.

YOU CAN'T SEPARATE THE MESSAGE FROM THE MESSENGER

Business today is increasingly personal. Sure, many of our meetings and communications happen virtually. Yet more than ever, outcomes are directly tied to our personality and communication style. Simply put—do people like you? Trust you? Want to do business with you?

A story binds the message to the messenger.

People want to know your story; they want to know who you are. We have code words for the values that sort of person who can communicate to the world: passionate, authentic, charismatic. When you know yourself, your stories telegraph your own values loud and clear. For example, the best stories communicate trust without you having to actually say, "Trust me" (which invariably has the opposite, counteracting effect). There's nothing more seductive than someone who knows who they are.

I didn't always know how to express myself. In fact, for most of my 20s, I still felt like that same awkward chubby kid fresh off the boat from Switzerland. Except now I was navigating the world of business and social change. And despite my share of early success, I would often find myself tongue-tied and twisted in the high-stakes moments when everything hung in the balance.

One time, I must have been about 23 years old, I went to a late-night meeting with my cofounder and mentor, Nick. I had spent a week preparing for this presentation. Our projects were behind schedule and I was afraid we wouldn't deliver against our investors' expectations. Nick was rather preoccupied that night (he also ran another startup) and didn't have much time or patience for me. His aggravation made me freeze. I began to stammer as I tried to get the words out of my mouth. It got so bad that I was literally choking on my tongue.

Next thing I knew, I was on the floor coughing, gasping for air, and thinking I was going to die in Conference Room D. Eventually, I recovered, though my embarrassment haunted me for weeks. Why was I so good with words and ideas, except in situations where my audience didn't seem to care or was downright dismissive? All my mojo would go right out the window. It was as if there was an invisible force at play, a kryptonite to my ability to influence and persuade.

After that night, I decided I never wanted to feel that way again. I needed to figure this out. How to communicate anything new, different, or disruptive to a resistant audience. You could say that my journey with storytelling began that fateful night.

The heart of the storyteller becomes the heart of the story.

If your message is personal to you, you have a much better chance of making it personal to your audience. If you're emotionally invested in your ideas, your audience will equate that to motivation, resilience, and long-term achievement. We are all imperfect beings. Let your vulnerabilities be seen, and you're far more likely to engender trust and rapport.

If, on the other hand, you're not personally invested in your story, that emotional absence creates a vacuum. Before you know it, that vacuum will be filled. If your audience feels you're disconnected and disembodied from your message, they will take you to task for it. If they sense an unresolved and unacknowledged inner conflict, they will naturally be wearier and standoffish. Or they will tell the story for you in a way you don't recognize. Think celebrity tabloids and how they take some small grain of truth from a story and twist it to their own ends. In other words, if you're not telling the story, someone is going to tell it for you. You're always better off taking control of your own narrative. Even if you feel that you're still a work in progress. We all are.

The best leaders share stories about *themselves*. That's what makes others believe in them. I know one investor who's backed an entrepreneur six times despite losing his money every time. Why? Because he believes in this person. And one of his small bets is going to eventually pay off. He just knows it. Maybe one day it will. That sort of blind faith investment only happens when people know your story.

In his book *Pour Your Heart Into It*, former Starbucks chairman and CEO Howard Schultz explained how he raised $1.65 million from 30 different investors to fund his first coffee enterprise, Il Giornale. (Starbucks and Il Giornale became one when Schultz bought Starbucks in 1987.) Schultz's story was disruptive at the time, and many potential investors turned him down. They thought the idea was crazy, that no one would be interested in buying Italian-style espresso drinks. But Schultz refused to give up. He kept telling his story. Writes Schultz, "If you ask any of those investors today why they took the risk, almost all of them would tell you that they invested in me, not in my idea. They believed because I believed, and they prospered because they trusted someone in whom nobody else had confidence."[1]

Now, as Howard Schultz runs for president of the United States in the 2020 election cycle, he is sharing the story of his growing up in public housing. How his father, a returning GI from World War II, was injured at work, and without health insurance or disability benefits, their family struggled to pay the bills. This early defining experience greatly influenced Schultz's personal philosophy and corporate policies at Starbucks, which became the first major American corporation to offer health insurance benefits to part-time employees. We are all the product of our early experiences and the choices that we made in response to what happened to us.

Story is the glue that forms relationships, professional and personal alike. You've probably been hired for your own story. If you were an appealing narrator on your first-round job interview, you made it to the next round, and from there into an office. Careers begin, progress, and often end based on the *story*.

If I asked you, "Where did your spouse grow up?" or "What's one of the hardest struggles your parents went through?" you'd have stories to tell. If I asked about your best customers, your

Exercise: Discovering Your Superhero Origins

Superheroes capture our imaginations for a reason. Think of your personal favorites: Black Panther, Wonder Woman, Iron Man. They each have an epic origin story of how they came into their powers. Few superheroes are *born* superheroes. It's through trials and circumstances, and the choices they make in response, that they discover who they truly are.

Take Bruce Wayne, for example. He was a young child of seven when he saw his parents murdered by a mugger in a dark alley. In that moment, he vowed to spend the rest of his life (and his family's fortune) to right the scales of justice. It took him years of searching, training, and mentoring to find and fulfill his rightful destiny as Batman. Gotham would never be the same.

Okay, you're not a superhero. Neither am I.

But every one of us has an epic origin story of how we came to see the world as we do.

The author and anthropologist Simon Sinek reminds us to "start with why." Why do you do what you do? Why are you where you are today? Why are you passionate about it?

To tell your *why* story without sounding self-indulgent, you must take the ordinary and celebrate the extraordinary within it.

Explore the following questions:

- Where were you born and raised?
- Who were your parents?
- What have you studied in life?

- What have you been most curious about?
- What have been the biggest risks you've taken?
- What are three to five of the most defining moments in your life?
- What about your early origins explains your why today?
- What do you geek out on? What are your hobbies/interests?

Take 10 to 15 minutes to write out your answers. You'll be surprised by what emerges.

We often forget to connect the dots about where we come from and how our early experiences shape how we see the world and what motivates us. Don't worry if you don't get it perfect. In our storytelling workshops, we encourage people to share a 90-second story based on the material they uncover. But you could spend a lifetime decoding the tea leaves of your past.

The key is to simply celebrate the gifts of your origins. Whether it's been easy, or more likely full of struggle and challenges to overcome, there is power in your past. In fact, the greatest source of untapped power is the part of your story that is unreconciled. Try to make friends with the twists and turns. No story is ever a straight line.

workmates, your favorite boss, odds are that you have lots of stories to share about them as well.

And the opposite also applies. If there are no shared stories or experiences of any kind connecting you with others, good luck making the relationship, friendship, or collaboration last.

THE OUTSIDER AS CULTURAL HERO

Your backstory is uniquely yours. But chances are you have something in common with most other innovators (including me). In some way, you've spent your life feeling different from others.

Being an outsider is an archetypal role for anyone on the journey of disruption. When you're a changemaker, you are—by definition—working outside the norm. Of course, you stand apart from others. Of course, your ideas are different. And, of course, that sucks and isn't easy.

Once upon a time, it was a rare individual who dared step outside the bounds of the culture to question what everybody else considered to be absolute truth. To do so was to defy the gods, to be a heretic. It could be dangerous, resulting in loss of limb or tongue, excommunication, or, worse yet, an excruciating death by fire or stoning. It was a lot safer to conform to the beliefs and groupthink of your clan, faith, or community.

Even a few decades ago, when I was a kid, being different was a sort of death sentence. Not a literal one but a social one. I was the boy no one wanted to sit with at lunch. Maybe you were picked on by the mean girls. The age of disruption has changed all that. Now, being a nerd isn't so bad! Just ask Bill Gates or Hermione Granger. Outsider status can be a point of pride of epic proportions. If you question the received wisdom and the norms of society, you are

"The myth is the public dream and the dream is the private myth. If your private myth, your dream, happens to coincide with that of society, you are in good accord with your group. If it isn't, you've got an adventure in a dark forest ahead of you."

JOSEPH CAMPBELL

no longer branded a heretic. You are a cultural hero. Assuming, you can get your message across.

Never before has the dominant culture lionized the disruptor—the innovator, the maverick, and the revolutionary—in the way we do today. College admissions officers are on the lookout for young people who think for themselves. Job recruiters seek out creatives, people who exude uniqueness and individuality. Our diverse, entrepreneurial society preaches that you can be anybody you want to be, do anything you want to do. No need to follow the pack. Everybody's a leader, right?!

And yet...

One thing hasn't changed. When you are pushing innovation, you're still questioning what others perceive as truth and reality. You're still daring to redefine boundaries and norms. Like Prometheus, you are stealing fire from the gods, and that carries a great risk and cost. You may not be chained to a rock, only to have your liver devoured by an eagle every day, but it's serious just the same.

Today's culture is obsessed with the outsider—the underdog. The David-versus-Goliath story. But let's be honest. Throughout history, 99 percent of the time Goliath wins. The established order is a formidable body that treats disruptors like a foreign virus, to be destroyed by the antibodies of society. Culture is programmed for self-preservation. It's just doing its job.

How can you narrow the odds of failure? How can you offer your radical ideas to insiders and not only keep your limbs and life but, better yet, be welcomed with open arms?

It took me years to answer these questions. For a long time, I felt exiled, like Odysseus, a long way from home. Never quite belonging to any of the cultures that I lived in, from Switzerland to Washington, DC. Yet in fairness, I was not a victim. I chose to listen to a calling, as every quest requires. As a result, I *had* to get in touch with my own story. I had to accept that the very differences that kept me outside the village walls could become my greatest gifts. In fact, these early experiences are what fueled my obsession with communications and culture-making. As one of my favorite sayings goes, "We teach what we need to learn most."

BEING RIGHT WITHOUT MAKING OTHERS WRONG

Is your life defined by not fitting in? If so, your identity will be rooted in struggle, defiance, and challenge. The inciting incidents that made you a change agent—your early trauma, your professional disappointment, your privileged upbringing, your crushed ideals—while they are great gifts, can also be the biggest obstacles to your success. The drive to innovate is usually born out of rejection by others. Yet those others are the very people your work is meant to reach.

Seth Godin, a prolific author on the spread of ideas, puts it this way: "Every person in the market has a worldview when it comes to what you're selling... When your story aligns with my worldview, we have something to discuss. When it doesn't, you're likely to be invisible."[2]

Or worse, cast out, shunned, and ignored.

That is the conundrum of being a changemaker. You bring forward a new story, filled with untapped potential. But your audience still lives in the old story. To them, your new worldview makes no sense. It's weird, different, a personal affront. It challenges their worldview, and that can make them feel bad, stupid, or just plain *wrong*.

To sell your disruptive ideas, you have to find a way to return to the insider culture that you rejected—or that rejected you—with an offering that they will receive and embrace.

And you have to do it without making the insiders feel that they are wrong. That's when the golden moment comes, and your worldviews align. You're an outsider, a rebel, a maverick, a threat, but suddenly everyone says, *Wait! You have what we want.* You belong.

The offering that you bring back from your journey is an *Undeniable Story*. In the next chapter, we'll learn more about how to structure that story, so it doesn't make your audience feel wrong.

But first, you need to get in touch with the part of yourself that is going to make the journey.

TURNING YOUR STRUGGLES INTO SOMETHING MORE

Let's be clear, you're not telling your personal story here for the sake of catharsis or therapy. You're doing it to get in touch with

"When the culture is in trouble, it calls back the outsiders."

CAROLINE CASEY

your natural authority. To access the power within required to complete this mythic quest. If you dare to do something as bold as rewriting reality, stealing fire from the gods, and challenging the established order, people are going to ask, *Who do you think you are? And what gives* you *the right?*

The struggle and pain of being an outsider may well be what motivates you. But no one is drawn to a disruptor who's fueled by anger, resentment, or revenge. Your ideas won't get far if you're always subconsciously saying "F you" to the world. Trust me, I've tried: it doesn't work. The passions that drive you, the struggles that forge you, the pain that propels you—you have to reconcile all of these forces within yourself. To tell your personal story is to make meaning of your life, and that includes your life's struggles.

Few have written as powerfully about the meaning of life than Viennese psychiatrist Viktor Frankl. In *Man's Search for Meaning*, one of the bestselling books of all time, Frankl shares his firsthand account of the Auschwitz concentration camp during the Holocaust. He witnessed unspeakable acts—both of darkness, and of humanity. Having survived the inconceivable, Frankl devoted the rest of his life to making sense of this experience and developing logotherapy, a psychotherapeutic approach.

Witnessing the darkest shadow of humanity, Frankl was eager to understand how he and some of his fellow death camp prisoners managed to live to tell the tale. It somehow seemed to be more than just luck. He noticed it was those who found the will to live in the face of the daily brutality. Those who could make a meaningful story out of their suffering (e.g., just the possibility of being reunited with their beloved) were the ones who found the strength and hope to live another day.

I truly hope that no one reading this book has ever had to endure such tragic cruelty. Yet each of us, in our own way, has struggled. Suffering is not a contest. Whatever hardships you have faced, they are real and personal to you. It's how you narrate your suffering that matters. This is a fateful choice.

Odds are, if you can make a meaningful story of it, one in which you are not the victim of your circumstances, you have the power to reclaim your narrative. That is the redemptive arc of life, and what makes your struggle relatable and accessible to others. Nobody wants to meet you in your victimhood; we want to know that you've had to overcome challenges in your life, as we have too.

Bill Gates's first business—Traf-O-Data—was a failure. Star surfer Bethany Hamilton's arm was bitten off by a shark. Stephen King's first book (*Carrie*) was rejected 30 times. J.K. Rowling's first book was rejected by 12 publishers before the 13th (Bloomsbury) accepted it. She was on welfare when she wrote *Harry Potter and the Philosopher's Stone*.

Your life hasn't always been easy, and you've learned some things along the way. To be clear, you don't need to reveal your deepest and darkest secrets. Simply share the parts of your story that are relevant to the tasks, issues, or agenda at hand. What will make you more relatable?

DO YOU HAVE TO TELL YOUR PERSONAL STORY?

If you're asking people to go on an epic journey with you, they want and need to know who you are. What are you made of? How do you see the world? What are you willing to fight for?

If you're asking people to enter your world, *you* need to know who you are and how you comes across. You need to understand how to turn your quirks and idiosyncrasies into unique, appealing attributes. When your audience is rooting for you,

you'll be amazed at how much more forgiving they are of your imperfections.

And if you're asking people to see, feel, and believe the same things you do, they want and need to know your motivations. Why is this work so personal to you? Why are you a champion of it? What gives you the right to tell this story? Why should we trust you? Your own story is tied tightly to your natural authority to frame the narrative and lead us forward. Without this, your audience will smell a fake from a mile away.

Your personal story is the engine that propels your *Undeniable Story*. So, yes, you have to tell it. How do you begin? By taking inventory of your life experiences. I like to make this more fun by asking you to think about superheroes. The exercise earlier in this chapter takes you through the steps.

If you ask anyone who really knows me, they will tell you that I'm obsessed with chocolate. I literally have a second fridge just for chocolate. Filled with kilos of single origin, craft chocolate bars. Many are rare, exotic, limited-edition bars—made from heirloom cacao grown in the tropics of Peru, Ecuador, São Tomé, Hawaii, and the Philippines to name a few.

Don't worry, I like to share. In fact, for years, I've hosted chocolate-tasting parties, soirees, and networking events, sharing my passion for the world's best chocolate with anyone willing to indulge. My social media bio states that "I'm left-handed, color-blind, and eat more chocolate than the average human." Not a week goes by that I don't get a tweet or email from somone who uses chocolate as the natural icebreaker or conversation starter. Everybody loves chocolate.

Recently, I went so far as to launch Choco Libre, a secret society for the world's greatest lovers of chocolate. It's the ultimate exercise in storytelling. A luxury chocolate subscription and social club with VIP tastings, brand activations, corporate gifting, and other ridiculousness. All based on my passion for chocolate, storytelling, and community building.

In our Storied workshops, we teach a technique we call *StorySparks* to get participants to reflect on their life and career experiences, then share a 90-second story with a partner. People are often moved to tears as they recognize the influences and defining moments that have made them into who they are. They also make unexpected connections that deepen their bond and sense of shared experience with the partner in the exercise. In less than two minutes, their sense of self and the world gets redefined. That's the magic of storytelling. If you can open yourself to people and allow them to connect with your story, you build an incredible bridge of trust.

YOU HAVE YOUR STORY—NOW WHAT?

I know. Talking about yourself may be the last thing you want to do. In our corporate training and workshops, I've heard every objection you can think of.

- "I don't have a story. Am I supposed to make something up?"
- "I'm not that interesting. Who wants to hear about me?"
- "I'd rather focus on the stories of those we serve than my own chest beating."
- "It's a distraction from the business at hand."
- "It's not about me. I'd rather let the product [company, result, etc.] speak for itself."

This reluctance is normal. I've struggled with it myself. It took me years to be able to tell my own story, and even now it doesn't

"The truth is: Belonging starts with self-acceptance. Your level of belonging, in fact, can never be greater than your level of self-acceptance, because believing that you're enough is what gives you the courage to be authentic, vulnerable, and imperfect."

———

BRENÉ BROWN

always come easy. Yet there is always a payoff to inviting people into your personal story.

The more I've learned about the narrative mindset, the more this truth has become evident: the self is the starting point for all stories. The heart of the storyteller becomes the heart of the story.

A few years ago, I published a post on my blog titled "You Are a Storyteller, and You Have a Story Worth Telling." The post generated a lot of discussion, but I was most taken with Jim Signorelli's comment: "Yes, we all have a story. However, for many of us, we never realize its full potential. That's because it's hidden underneath what we often think is our story, but in truth it is nothing more than a resume—a plot with no emotional significance."[3]

As you may have guessed by now, I'm convinced we all have an emotionally significant personal story within us. Probably more than one. It's a matter of digging it out, dusting it off, and putting it to use. Once you identify and make sense of your own personal story, what do you do with it? How does your backstory tie in to the *Undeniable Story* you need to tell for your work?

1   **It tears down walls:** Audiences can sense when there's a wall between an organizational story and its narrator. Don't build walls. Tear them down. Let people see why your work matters to you. Zeroing in on what's personal to you in your work makes you a more relatable, more believable storyteller.

2   **It shows presence and ownership:** As I mentioned earlier, business is increasingly personal. Audiences tend to look for and believe in the person behind the narrative. If you and your story aren't there, your audience will read that as a lack of embodiment and ownership. If you are personally present and own your story, you will telegraph passion and conviction.

3   **It makes the conceptual real:** As you'll learn in Part II of this book, crafting an *Undeniable Story* can be a conceptual process.

To keep the story from becoming abstract, it's good to start with story elements that are concrete. That means telling what you know best. And what you know best is typically the story you have lived.

At what point should you weave your personal story into your work narrative? That depends. You can introduce your story at any of the three steps you'll learn about in Part II.

It can become part of the context for change, forming part of your origin story. Explaining how you came to recognize the new possibility you are championing. It can boost the story's emotion, maybe illustrating a struggle you've witnessed between what someone wants and what gets in their way. Or it can become part of the evidence of truth, describing the journey you've been on, for instance, and reinforcing the expertise you've built up along the way.

Where you introduce your personal backstory, and how much of that story you tell, depends on who your audience is and how you want to affect them. Before we can talk about that, we need to look more closely at how story affects the 21st-century brain, heart, and body. Storytelling is what moves us and feeds us.

"People will forget
what you said, people
will forget what you
did, but people will
never forget how you
made them feel."

MAYA ANGELOU

3

The Feel-Good Principle

IN THIS CHAPTER

- On the matter of feeling good

- Why we are wired for narrative

- How to avoid the data trap

- The neurobiology of storytelling

- How big narrative trumps big data

- The Feel-Good Principle in action

MY DAD, GEOFF, is a legend in the food industry (though he would never say as much). He's a chemical engineer by training and an inventor by trade. He and his team invented Nestlé's Swiss Water process for naturally decaffeinating coffee. He also invented the holy grail of veggie burgers years before startups like Beyond Meat and Impossible Foods raised hundreds of millions in venture capital. Today, he's the chief scientist for Califia Farms, a leading almond milk and plant-based food company in the United States.

My father has been on a lifelong quest to make food better—healthier, more wholesome, and tastier. Yet the inventor's life is never easy. Many of his breakthrough ideas didn't always find the success they deserved. Like that holy grail of veggie burgers. It was high in protein and low in fat and calories. In blind taste tests (without the bun, lettuce, tomato, and special sauce), people couldn't tell the difference between his plant-based burger and a regular beef burger. He and his business partners struggled to sell their concept. They landed meetings with the biggest burger chains and fast-casual restaurants in the country. My dad spent hours practicing his pitch. But, in meeting after meeting, the response was the same: "Interesting... but the historical data doesn't prove our customers want this." Sound familiar?

They all said no. Nobody would buy what my dad was selling.

When he was ready to sell the vision of a game-changing healthy burger, my dad faced obstacle after obstacle. He was ahead of his time. Executives at the national restaurant chains just weren't ready for a healthy burger. Not yet. There was one other problem: a master pitchman my father is not. Granted, he's a genius (I may be biased). Though, like a typical engineer, he believes his products speak for themselves. Just taste it! The truth is on his side. Except he couldn't overcome the cultural forces and barriers at the time.

Here's the thing about innovative ideas. To the innovator—people like my dad, like *you*—it is an amazing new solution that will blow people's minds (and maybe their taste buds). But audiences don't see it that way. For audiences, the very same idea questions or challenges what they know to be true or are comfortable with.

Think about the ultimate purpose of your story. You didn't get into the game of being an innovator or disruptor to maintain the status quo. You're driven to question it. The problem is when you challenge the "old ways," you trigger people's fight-flight-freeze response. This is especially the case when the old ways were built, cherished, or championed by the very people in your audience. So, for your *Undeniable Story* to have the impact you desire, you have to understand something about how our brains are wired. What repels versus what creates a receptive field.

What turns us off. And what turns us on.

THE FEEL-GOOD PRINCIPLE

As with many other members of the animal kingdom, we like things that make us feel good. We avoid stuff that hurts, feels bad, or is painful. It's a basic biological principle: embrace pleasure, avoid pain. It's one of the wisest parts of our survival instinct.

I call this the *Feel-Good Principle*. If you want to transform how the world thinks about your product, cause, or message, try making people feel *better* about themselves. Rather than making them feel like crap. Let's face it, as it is, most of us are already overloaded with feeling bad. Life can often feel like a giant pile of suck, with a massive stack of problems coming at us from every direction.

Most leaders have people bringing them problems every day—all day long. Complaints about coworkers. Complaints about customers and suppliers. Complaints about complaints. The list goes on. Adding one more problem to the pile is not always welcome. The *real* boss move is to come bearing a positive, feel-good story of possibility and opportunity. A VP once confessed to me how he just pines for a meeting where someone brings him good news, something inspiring and exciting that he could champion and get behind. Instead he was being asked to fix and clean up other people's messes.

This makes so much intuitive sense. Who wouldn't choose to feel good instead of feeling bad? Yet, this flies in the face of what most of us have been taught about selling or promoting a new idea. We've been taught that we should focus on what's wrong, what's missing. To diagnose the problem and provide the solution. Tell people they're wrong and show them what's right. "Invent the disease and offer the pill," as the adage goes in advertising. It's what storytelling expert Jonah Sachs, in his book *Winning the Story Wars*, describes as "inadequacy marketing."

For the last 70 years, we've been taught to believe that the only way to market products is to make people feel bad. Tell them they have a problem, then offer the solution. Bad breath? This minty-fresh gum will solve that. Boring car? This brand-new convertible will perk you up. Nowadays, however, we're seeing this 20th-century best-practice for advertising and marketing increasingly falls on deaf ears. Why?

Because we don't know who to trust and what to believe.

In Silicon Valley, disruption is a glorified term—everyone wants to be a disruptor. It's often unintentional, but if you look at the narrative structure of what and how you're communicating, it's all too easy to tell people, *You're wrong and you're stupid. But don't worry. I'm so much smarter than you. I have the answer. I'm going to fix things and make it all better.* Then we wonder why people don't love us and embrace our products in the way we need, hope, or expect them to.

Fortunately, there's a simple answer to this dilemma. Give people faith in the future. More than anything, that's what people are looking for from their leaders and from the vendors or solution providers they buy from. They want to know, at the end of the day, that there's a better future ahead. And you're the one who needs to paint that picture. With an *Undeniable Story* that is difficult if not impossible to resist.

The true power of story is that you always have the power to reinterpret past experiences from a new vantage point. This is one of the most important skills that leaders and entrepreneurs must learn in terms of this language of storytelling. We're constantly having to shift, change, adapt, pivot, reinvent. When the world changes—and it does, constantly—you have to change your story. When *you* change, your *story* must change to reflect your new world. Each time you go through change, you have to recalibrate your own story for better coherence and resonance. Retell and reinterpret your story from a new vantage point in a way that serves the new future.

WIRED FOR NARRATIVE

Researchers have found that while 90 percent of people say that a strong narrative in a presentation is critical for them to feel

"If I ask you to think about something, you can decide not to. But if I make you feel something? Now I have your attention."

———————

LISA CRON

engaged by it, 46 percent of presenters say that the hardest part of creating a successful presentation is crafting a compelling story.[4]

You might think you suck at storytelling. I'm here to tell you that you can do this. Anyone can. Even my dad the engineer has come to appreciate his natural ability to craft a story. You can be shy, geeky, and introverted. More analytical than creative. You can still tell a compelling story. The trick comes from *thinking* in narrative.

You're actually hardwired for it. The ability to make stories is quite literally a part of your DNA. Scientists have identified a specific gene, FOXP2, that they call the storytelling gene. Unless you have a rare brain disorder, you have this gene, and it's turned on. You were born ready to story.

Every experience, every object, every relationship is stored in the mind with a story attached to it. FOXP2 is a gene that activates the cognitive function for meaning-making. It influences how we make sense of everything that shows up in our lives. If you want to unlock meaning and motivation with any audience, tell them a story that reflects the future they seek and identify with.

Our storytelling instincts are what separate us from all other species. Daniel Gilbert, a Harvard professor of social psychology, speaks about our unique ability to tell stories. In his international bestseller, *Stumbling on Happiness*, he describes this defining human trait: *imagination*. Our ability to dream and envision, and to turn that seed into reality—this is what separates us from every other animal in the kingdom. Decades ago, the dream was for humanity to set foot on the moon. Today, the vision is for a clean-energy future. A solution to climate change. Or, god forbid, a piece of luggage you can ride around on at the airport.

Humans are neurologically hardwired to make sense of the world through story and narrative. It's our ability to envision something new and then convey it to others through story that is the superhero power of humanity. You have an idea, a vision, a dream. Then, through a series of words and actions that spark the imagination of others, it can become a *shared* dream. And from there, it can transform from thought into a manifested tangible reality. This is how every great thing has ever been built. The very foundations of human civilization. From the Egyptian pyramids to Nutella (arguably one of the greatest inventions ever).

Our audience has questions. They need answers. Do we share stories in common? Do we see the world the same way? Can I trust you as my fellow brother or sister, or are you a threat to my survival? Are you friend or foe? Am I safe, or will you eat me? You'd be surprised how often this script is unconsciously running in the background of our audience's minds, whether in the executive boardroom, at a press conference, or a congressional hearing. The very foundations of identity, tribe, and belonging are built upon narrative constructs.

The German beer-maker Heineken conducted an interesting experiment, summarized in a viral video titled "Worlds Apart." The experiment put pairs of diametrically opposed people together. For example, someone on the political right paired with someone on the political left. An avowed feminist with an anti-feminist. A refugee and a nationalist. Neither knew the other's beliefs or values. Heineken then ran each pair of people through a variety of team-building exercises. As they completed the exercises, these individuals naturally built bonds of friendship, respect, and camaraderie with each other. As the experiment ends, the beliefs and values of each member of the pair were revealed to the other. Heineken then gave the pairs the option: walk away or share a beer with their new acquaintance. Each pair decided to be friends and share a beer together (a Heineken, of course), despite their differences.

As a cultural anthropologist, I'm fascinated by the role storytelling has served in the foundation of every culture. For thousands of years, most of the stories we told were about preserving the social order. We had trusted authority figures (the shaman, the elder, the priest) who told us the stories of our lives. These were cautionary tales that taught us the correct behavior and the proper order of things. How to be safe. How to contribute meaningfully to the tribe. *This is how we hunt buffalo. Don't eat the purple berries. This water is safe to drink.* We literally owe our lives to these stories. In a brutal world where the tiger or tsunami could kill us, this is how we protected and preserved the village. Follow the rules. Because everyone's lives depend on it.

In contrast, today, most stories are about *questioning* and *challenging* the social order. *Think different. Be the change you want to see. Don't follow the trends; be the trendsetter.* We live in a very different age. Anyone can be the storyteller. In the words of the great social philosopher Clay Shirky, "Here comes everybody." Worldviews and value systems are colliding and transforming before our very eyes, faster than ever before. Which means the stories are literally up for grabs. Consequently, our primal wiring is stretched to the limit, but it's all we've got.

So, let's take a closer look at that wiring, and how we can use it to rewrite the script of how people respond to ideas that challenge the status quo.

THE DATA TRAP: DEAD ON ARRIVAL

TL;DR. Too long; didn't read. It's a common acronym in internet culture.

I've coached many leaders under pressure to provide a TL;DR summary for their boss. Basically, it's shorthand for "give me the bottom line." Just get to the data and conclusions. Skip the fluff.

Exercise: Ahead of Your Time

The challenge that you may face when inventing the future is that you're ahead of your time. People don't believe the data you have to show. People are afraid to leave behind the comfort of the status quo. Why? Because the existing storyline, the dominant thought of the time, has too strong a hold on their beliefs.

Take a moment to think about your answers to these questions:

- When have you felt ahead of your time?
- Have you ever struggled to describe something so obvious to you, yet everyone else stares at you with suspicion or disbelief?
- How can you frame your story in a way that will be embraced instead of rejected?

Modern business management reinforces this adage. Time is money. So, let's get to the answer. And give me the data.

Except it's not such a wise strategy if your answer questions the established order.

Think back to what happens when you lead with data and conclusions. Too often, your story is dead on arrival. The typical responses include...

- "Well, how exactly did you come up with that data?"
- "I still don't believe it."
- "I have a different interpretation."

"Science is not opposed to storytelling. Science is a genre of storytelling. Stories of the real world, inspired by observations thereof."

SEAN CARROLL

People are naturally suspicious of anything that challenges their existing beliefs.

And the next thing you know, you're on the defensive. You're facing an adversarial audience, and they simply don't care or believe in your data and conclusions. Instead of being in control of the narrative, you failed the 90 percent test. You may even be further back then when you started.

Many executives face this quandary during the ritual of quarterly business reviews (QBRs). Every 90 days, they are required to present their vision, roadmap, and metrics to senior management to justify their progress and performance. A Fortune 500 client started working with us after delivering a disastrous review. The executive began his presentation by apologizing for disappointing results in the previous quarter, outlining why his team hadn't "bent the curve" and met overambitious expectations. He figured, *Let's get the bad news out of the way first so we can get to the good news.*

Except the meeting wasn't long enough to get to the good news. Instead, senior management spent three-quarters of the time dressing down the executive in a post-mortem. And there had been so much opportunity to share and celebrate where things were headed next.

This is what happens when you lose control of the narrative.

This leader's credibility was badly tarnished. His reputation sullied. Within weeks, his career path had stalled and he was "layered." Passed up for a promotion, and a new boss put in over him. However, within six months after we started working with him, he was back on the right track. He regained his standing and had the right narrative to dramatically influence the future of the company.

So, how do you get to the heart of your message quickly? Even when you don't yet have all the data and numbers to validate your vision? That's the reality of innovation, and why so many of us struggle with presenting it. When you're doing something that's new or never been done before, you rarely have all the empirical data to prove it—before you do it. So, you have to speak about a better future. Find a way to make people feel good. Remind them of the possibilities. It also means you have to take a leap and find ways to test and verify. By collecting experiential data that proves out your intuition, and dialing-in or course-correcting the vision vector. This makes for an iterative story.

Talk to a typical head of any business unit and you'll quickly hear how they are drowning in a sea of data. Every business is in the same boat. Struggling to make sense and meaning of all this data. There's no context. No emotional connection. Numbers are just numbers. The challenge is that our brains are quick to abstraction. Especially when a number set goes beyond that which our eyes can see (say, a few thousand). Yet, increasingly, your data stories involve millions, if not billions, of data points; those are often the stories we must tell. In the age of big data, with infinite data sets, we can quickly lose the plot and get overwhelmed with what data to present, much less what story to tell. In the end, it's the story behind the numbers that matters most.

I'm not suggesting that you shouldn't use data. By all means! A presentation without supporting data is like a sandwich with two fat slices of bread and nothing between. A lot of empty carbs yet not truly satisfying.

The issue is with *when* and *where* you use the data. In business, we are taught to "lead with data." But when you start with numbers, your story is dead on arrival. It prompts the audience to question your story and pick it apart. *Says who? Where did you get your figures?* It's all open to interpretation.

When you start with data and conclusions, you signal to your audience that the story is over. As Kevin Roberts reminds us, "The essential difference between emotion and reason is that emotion leads to action and reason leads to conclusion." Since the story is about to end, you're inviting your audience to question and challenge the data and conclusions. Especially if what you're proposing challenges current assumptions. They may not be ready to accept what's been proposed, at least not the way it's been presented so far.

The moment you instigate your audience into questioning and challenging, you've put them into a stressful state: fight or flight. Instead of being open to your message, they're on the defensive.

Try the following alternative. Instead of data and conclusions, start with a timeless truth. Follow up with the questions related to that truth in a changing world and a changing context. Doing this brings us back to the feel-good sandwich.

YOUR BRAIN ON STORY

A good story can make our spirit soar and our heart skip a beat. This is no accident. When something captures our attention, like a problem, a conflict, or a threat, our brain sends out a signal to the rest of the body. My colleague Kendall Haven created the first detailed, tested model of dynamic story architecture that accounts for the neurology of how narrative material is processed, understood, remembered, and recalled in a receiver's mind. His two seminal works (*Story Proof* and *Story Smart*) have revolutionized our understanding of the neural and science aspects of effective story structure and outline his major advances in story and narrative theory.

Pay attention to the messages your brain sends to your body. As part of its survival instinct programming, our body is prepared to respond, to escape a perceived threat. Adrenaline will surge into our bloodstream, immediately kicking us into gear. This powerful compound boosts our attention, strength, and speed. Our pulse races, beads of sweat drip down our backs, and we are on full alert, acutely aware of our surroundings. Exciting, right?

Yet, here's the thing. If our brains continue to perceive a threat, then the second phase of the hormonal cascade begins. Fight, flight, or freeze. Cortisol, also known as the "stress" hormone, is released into our bloodstream. Cortisol keeps our bodies ready to fight or flee, but if it the reaction isn't relieved, the result is stress. The same stress we feel when we're up against a deadline, stuck in the traffic jam from hell, or caught up in an escalating argument.

Oxytocin is a completely different animal. Dubbed the "belonging" molecule, this hormone is released when we feel deep emotional connection and intimate communion. A great meal, a perfect sunset, a passionate lover. It's also scientifically proven to flow when consuming dark chocolate. We can all rejoice. Oxytocin is most pronounced in the bloodstream of parents of a newborn child. Such intelligent design. We are evolutionarily programmed to experience overwhelming feelings of love and devotion when in the company of a baby. Or chocolate. What a beautiful universe.

So therein lies, within any good story, the echoes of the entire arc of the human experience. From our desperate struggle for survival to moments of transcendent bliss.

People Don't Buy the Product:
They Buy the Story That's Attached to It

There's an American TV show called *Pawn Stars* on the History Channel. It's one of my TV guilty pleasures. Maybe you've watched it before?

Three generations of a family-owned business, the 24-hour Gold & Silver Pawn Shop, all working together in Las Vegas, Nevada. There's Old Man, the cranky grandfather. There's Rick Harrison, the boss in charge. There's his son, Corey, a 20-something slacker. And there's Chumlee, Corey's best friend, sidekick, and comedic relief.

It's like PBS's *Antiques Roadshow,* but a lot cooler.

Every episode centers on a series of potential customers who bring in an object they want to sell or pawn. We find out the story about the item. In some cases, they call in an expert for a consult to authenticate the object and provide a valuation. The two parties then negotiate to see if they can strike a deal. It makes for entertaining television.

Let's take a Zippo lighter, for example.

SCENARIO 1: An ordinary Zippo metal lighter—nothing special (worth about $20).

SCENARIO 2: A World War II Zippo lighter with the insignia of the 101st Airborne division (worth about $200).

SCENARIO 3: A monogrammed World War II Zippo lighter once owned by General George Patton (worth about ... priceless).

Same physical object, yet three different stories result in three completely different valuations. We don't buy the product: we buy the story that's attached to it. And even if I told you that the General Patton lighter is worth $3,000—and had an expert verify its worth—and then I offered it to you for just $1,000, would you be ready to buy it?

Why not?

Odds are because the Zippo lighter's story doesn't mean much to you. Sure, it's worth a few thousand dollars. Except you're not a Zippo collector. And you're not a World War II memorabilia collector. You wouldn't know where or how to find an interested buyer to resell it. Which means this story doesn't belong to you. It's not worth your time or attention.

We live in a culture that's obsessed with the numbers. But remember it's ultimately not about the numbers. It's the story behind the numbers that matters most—and whether it's a story that resonates and has meaning for your audience.

Paul J. Zak is a famed neuro-economist and a professor at Claremont Graduate University in Southern California. In his seminal research, he noticed that classic storytelling structure follows a predictable hormonal response: cortisol, then oxytocin. Think about it. A classic tale needs to capture your attention using some presenting drama or difficulty (cortisol). Then, at its conclusion, the classic tale leads to a happy ending (oxytocin). That made sense in simpler times when morality tales were how we learned the difference between right and wrong, how to contribute and belong to the tribe.

Yet think of your day-to-day life, the digital 21st-century cacophony in which we exist. The never-ending stream of your social media feeds. The 24-hour cable news cycle with constantly breaking reports of a world drowning in radical disruption and crisis after crisis. The incessant ping of text, email, Slack, and other notifications on your smartphone. It's a far cry from a relaxing evening around the fire, telling tales of the hunt and enjoying an infinite sky filled with stars.

Many of us are walking around in a chronic fog of cortisol-driven "fight or flight." We're perpetually trying to evaluate every incoming piece of information, to determine if its story is important to our survival. This is an old instinct stretched beyond utility. We need a new approach to storytelling for a new age of always-on communications. Perhaps that's why so many of us struggle with too much stress, too little sleep, and too much to do with far too little time. This dramatic change in our culture and lives invites us to consider a new perspective. Starting your story by triggering oxytocin is maybe the best influencing strategy for the new future you want to create.

THE MAGIC OF MIRROR NEURONS

Storytelling provides yet another biochemical response in us. Nicole Speers, Jeffrey M. Zacks, and a team of researchers discovered, using fMRI, that when people read stories, they build vivid mental simulations. As author Lisa Cron explains, it goes even deeper than that: "The areas of the brain that lit up when they *read* about an activity were identical to those that light up when they actually experience it... In short, when we read a story, we really do slip into the protagonist's skin, feeling what she feels, experiencing what she experiences."[5]

In other words, experiencing deep connections through story makes us feel the same way as experiencing those connections in real life. We can travel without moving. All through the power of a story that invites us to experience another world.

"The average daydream is about 14 seconds long and we have about 2,000 of them per day. In other words, we spend about half of our waking hours—one-third of our lives on Earth—spinning fantasies."

———

JONATHAN GOTTSCHALL

It turns out that these areas of the brain, inhabited by something called *mirror neurons*, fire not only when we perform a particular action but also when we see *someone else* perform the very same action—whether in reality or through story.

Storytelling is a virtual reality simulcast. In the act of great storytelling, mirror neurons start to fire in the audience in response to the teller's words. The audience mentally and vividly experiences what happens in the story. We experience a shared state or emotion. Vulcan mind meld in action! Bet you didn't think you'd be learning that trick in this book.

All communities are bound by their stories, and companies are no exception. We feel the structure of belonging in the digital age, building islands of identity to connect beyond geographical, economic, gender, class, and other boundaries. We defy the circumstances of our lives to meet and connect with others like us in Facebook groups, Meetups, Nextdoor, Twitch, and other online forums. A good story fires mirror neurons between the storyteller and the listener, developing a close bond with an audience in minutes.

But there's still a little more neurobiology to explore before we move on. Empathy—relating to another being beyond ourselves—is the product of a shared emotional experience.

THE OXYTOCIN-EMPATHY CONNECTION

Paul J. Zak has spent a considerable portion of his life studying the release of oxytocin in humans. He has also personally felt the effects of this powerful hormone.

One night, on a flight home, he watched the Oscar-winning film *Million Dollar Baby*. He was so moved by the film that he ended up crying so hard that everyone around him was painfully aware

"Stories create community, enable us to see through the eyes of other people, and open us to the claims of others."

PETER FORBES

of his distress. "The story was so engaging that it caused my brain to react as if I were a character in the movie," Zak recalled in a 2015 article for the journal *Cerebrum*. The experience was so profound that it prompted Zak to focus his studies of oxytocin on how the brain reacts to story.

Zak ran a series of experiments in which he had subjects watch videos, some of them emotionally engaging, others less so. Then he measured their feel-good oxytocin levels. He found that elevated oxytocin was linked with empathy. Writes Zak, "the change in oxytocin was associated with concern for the characters in the story... If you pay attention to the story and become emotionally engaged with the story's characters, then it is as if you have been transported into the story's world."

Immersion in an inspiring story and the accompanying spike in oxytocin result not just in empathy but in action. Zak found that people were far more likely to donate money after watching an emotionally charged, attention-getting story. "Narratives that cause us to pay attention and also involve us emotionally," he concluded, "are the stories that move us to action."

Studies like Zak's, the groundbreaking fMRI research of neuroscientists Read Montague and Matthew D. Lieberman, and the work of Daniel Kahneman and others show again and again the extent to which our rational minds are *not* in control of much of our decision-making. Instead, we are "mindless" bundles of emotions and hormones. Our brains light up in distinct and predictable areas when we are told different kinds of stories. These hormones create in us predictable emotions, which influence our beliefs and choice-making habits.

In short, the value of everything in life is based on the story we attach to it, and that is subjective to the beholder. This is the holy grail and magical aspect of storytelling unlocked in the 21st century.

BIG NARRATIVE TRUMPS BIG DATA

Even if you have the data, that doesn't mean you know how to tell a story about it.

Consider the following data story…

MRR = 73%. NPS = 62. COCA = $83. CLV = $335.

Unless you speak the alphabet soup of marketing metrics, you might have a hard time deciphering the story hiding behind acronyms and corresponding data. You might have an even harder time providing an interpretation of it. And therein lies the challenge.

MRR: monthly recurring revenue
NPS: net promoter score
COCA: cost of customer acquisition
CLV: customer lifetime value

Once we have the code, we understand. Assuming you speak the language of digital marketing. We are contextual creatures. We buy on emotion and then justify through logic.

If I don't have a context that I relate to in your message, if I don't personally identify with the desire and dilemma in your story, then I'll naturally question, deny, or discount your data. The opposite is also true. If I feel that you are in my tribe, that we share the same beliefs and motivations, then my confirmation bias and desire to conform to shared beliefs may trump any contradictory data.

We are all guilty of rejecting logical, rational sensible arguments every day.

Consider the political debate over climate change. Scientific, data-driven arguments are accepted or rejected based on which tribe people belong to. Not on whether or not the arguments are accepted by a majority of scientists. The challenge with climate change is that the story was too abstract for years, describing an end-state that seemed far removed from day-to-day reality. Now, with the dramatic rise of severe weather events, melting ice caps, and other environmental changes, it's becoming very real. Very fast. Yet it still sadly remains abstract and overwhelming to most. And thus the political will to truly make transformational 10x investments is lacking.

Here's the inconvenient truth. Our world 10 to 20 years from now will be dramatically different. We will most likely live on a planet where there are hundreds of millions, if not billions, of environmental and economic refugees. A mass migration of a magnitude never before seen as humans relocate from coastal cities and desolate farms to higher ground.

I shudder as I even write this.

So why can't we organize ourselves in advance of this inevitable future?

It feels rather doomsday talking about it, doesn't it? One of the most existential stories of our time: the potential self-annihilation of our species. Imagine what it must have felt like to live through the Black Death. Or World War II and the Holocaust. Imagine if social media had existed at those times. This is why learning to tell new and better life-affirming stories is such an important task. For the survival of our species.

It all comes down to storytelling. Today, solar and wind energy is cheaper to produce than coal. Electric vehicles are on the path to transform the transportation and energy economy of the world. There's a need for a lot more, a lot faster. And that's where being able to tell the aspirational story of a better world is so important; it brings to the life the benefits and use cases of new technological breakthroughs. Our future literally depends on it.

Perhaps the challenge with the climate change story is cortisol-induced fight, flight, or freeze—with a lot of flight or freeze. It's such a big story that many people feel powerless to change it.

So, what can we do? In the simplest of terms, choose a place you love, and take care of it. The more we feel connected to a place, the more inspired and invested we become in stewarding that place. We each need to find a place we want to love and care for on this planet.

If data is king, then context and emotion are queen. And it's always wise to let the queen go first. Context and emotion are the foundations of relationships and making meaning. Relevance is an emotionally based evaluation. If I feel that you are in my tribe, I am open to what you say. If not, I'll deny or discount your data. That's why people reject facts and logical arguments every day.

Data is not a bad thing. It's just not always a good opening gambit when you're trying to persuade a resistant audience to buy into a radical idea. It's not the feel-good sandwich your audience is hungry for. So, why aren't we taught to lead with emotion? Because emotions are unpredictable. They're soft and squishy.

They're human.

Mastering them will make you stronger.

Mastering them will make your case stronger.

Mastering them will make your story undeniable.

"Numbers numb, jargon jars, and nobody ever marched on Washington because of a pie chart."

ANDY GOODMAN

THE FEEL-GOOD PRINCIPLE IN ACTION

Let's get back to the main theme of this chapter: the Feel-Good Principle.

If we take the insights from neurobiology and combine them with the evolutionary context I described earlier, we have clues for how to create a better future.

When it comes to the act of selling innovation, we need to create a receptive field.

We tend to pay attention to the stories that make us feel good. We ignore the stories that make us feel bad, wrong, or stupid. Think about how this works in your own life. How often does an advertising pitch or self-help book resonate with you when it reminds you of how broken and messed up you are or, more simply, is designed to make you feel like sh*t? Guilt, shame, moralizing, self-righteousness, and pity don't make for a persuasive story.

The most human reaction is to get defensive, resist the message, or shut down. Fight, flight, or freeze.

So, when you open your presentation about change and disruption, you need to do so in a manner that makes people feel deeply connected (oxytocin). Help them to identify with the context you've presented, and in a way that makes them feel good. A way that offers hope for the future. Otherwise, they will bounce out of your story (too much cortisol) before you even have a chance to get to the happy ending.

So, how do you frame your story in a way that makes people feel good?

I devote the entire second half of this book to answering that question. With a clear structure and approach that you can bring to every high-stakes presentation. Your feel-good sandwich.

Here's a quick preview.

First, recognize the paradigm shift. We are living and working in extraordinary times. One that calls for an evolutionary leap in how we construct and tell our stories for the context of innovation. Help people see how the future already exists and the new, exciting potential that comes with change.

Second, take comfort in the "shared reality generator" function of storytelling. When those mirror neurons are at work, they can coax us into a common sensory experience. It's in those moments of shared meaning that deep bonding occurs. And it's how we can go from strangers to BFFs in a matter of just 60 seconds. It's where we discover the "invisible lines of connection," as Rabbi Lawrence Kushner describes them. All the ways that we are more similar than different.

In the next chapter, I'll outline the first step in crafting an *Undeniable Story*: See It. Getting others to see what you see is what we all long for, isn't it? To feel seen, heard, validated, accepted, and embraced in a shared experience of life.

PART II

CRAFTING AN UNDENIABLE STORY

"The future already exists, it's just not widely distributed."

———

WILLIAM GIBSON

4

Step 1: See It— The Context for Change

IN THIS CHAPTER

- **Getting others to see what you see**

- **Find your hook**

- **Name the change**

- **The convergence of forces**

- **Help your audience see the context for change**

WHAT IS THE structure of belonging in the digital age? That was the story we were asked to tell for one of the largest internet platforms in the world—how micro-tribes and communities can organize online. Imagine a product with 100 million power users that most people (much less, everyone inside the company) didn't understand—what it is, how it works, or what it can do for them. That was the challenge faced by the head of product of a not-so-small social media company. Here's an excerpt from the narrative we created:

> As technology evolves, humans are increasingly turning to digital solutions to enable our fundamental need to belong. For the entirety of human history, we've sought the places and people we belong with. Our family. Our tribe. Our community. We do this by connecting around the things we have in common. A goal (let's rebuild our town after disaster strikes). A life experience (I've just become a parent). A medical condition (people with cancer). The list goes on and on. In the past, belonging was limited to who you knew or where you lived. [Our product] allows you to belong anywhere you want. With whomever you want. The potential is limitless. It really does connect and unlock the world. What used to happen only in our neighborhoods, churches, bars, and local establishments increasingly happens online. The growth of [our product]

speaks to a profound sociological trend. People have a fundamental desire to find and connect with like-minded others online, whether it's related to politics, career, health, community, a hobby, or a life-changing event. To express both our public and private selves. We want to feel like we belong to something bigger. So, we wanted to share with you how, as a team, we've been thinking about the changing nature of belonging. And how this is driving our product vision/roadmap forward.

Like the organization we worked with, many companies are recognizing that despite their physical/digital product, at the end of the day, it's a sense of community and connection that people are seeking most. The structure of belonging is the future of business.

This is personal to me. I spent much of my life feeling like an outsider, someone who simply didn't belong anywhere. This experience colored my perception of the world, and my understanding of the stories around me. You might look at a dozen swatches of paint and naturally see the story in them that someone else doesn't. An accountant might look at a financial spreadsheet and immediately see that story. Even so, get three accountants in a room together, and each might have a different version or interpretation of what they see. You might see a novel solution to a problem that has stumped others for years. Innovation is built on the principle of seeing something that others don't yet see.

Vision. Insights. Revelations.

At the same time, you have to be constantly aware that, when it comes to change, where you feel at home, others might feel alone. In other words, where you see possibilities, others see danger.

As we explored in Part I, disruption is an unsettling prospect for most people. When you challenge someone's worldview, it's like suggesting they're wrong. This puts them on the defensive, encouraging an adversarial dynamic. It's no surprise that a typical response is reluctance, sometimes even straight-up resistance, or downright defiance.

Instead of challenging your audience's worldview, give them something to connect with. Something to have faith in. *Show them a destination they want to go to, then help them see it the way you do.* If the destination you've shown them is inspiring enough, compelling enough, intriguing enough, then they will willingly—perhaps even enthusiastically—follow you there.

Story, as we're about to see, is both a location device and a transportation vehicle. *Where is this story taking us? Do we want to go there? How do we get there?* Help your audience locate themselves in the narrative, then show them the promised land.

GETTING OTHERS TO SEE WHAT YOU SEE

To you, the future is clear.

It's undeniable, irresistible, and inevitable to your eyes. You're so excited about this vision that you can't contain yourself.

You want *everyone* to see what you see.

You want *everyone* to be as excited about your vision as you are.

You want *everyone* to see it, feel it, and believe it—like you do.

There's just one thing. Only *you* are you. *No one else* is.

We all have different neurological wiring, different life experiences, different perceptions of the world around us. The way I see myself and the world around me is probably different from the way others see me and the world around them.

The first step in getting others to see what you see is to appreciate that no one else perceives what you do in exactly the same way. The next step is to realize that while you can't control others'

"If you want to build a ship, don't drum up people to collect wood and don't assign them tasks and work, but rather teach them to long for the endless immensity of the sea."

ANTOINE DE SAINT-EXUPÉRY

perceptions, you can influence what people see and feel—and in turn what they choose to believe. When you tell an *Undeniable Story*, you can redefine the frame and turn the impossible into the inevitable.

Instead of trying to push your views onto your audience, welcome them into a new and exciting world. Many may feel like tourists at first, so you must play the tour guide. They are travelers in a foreign land who don't speak the language. Perhaps they can't even understand the road signs. Your job is to make them feel at home. Narrate the landscape. Point out the sights. Give them the inside scoop, the local insider knowledge.

Notice how the best tour guides are always the greatest storytellers.

Your job is to help your audience see the world from a fresh perspective. To discover the invisible lines of connection that tie a vision of the future to their own past. And, once they see the lines of connection, to place themselves within that future vision. To adopt it as their own story.

Yet, remember the world that you live and breathe 24/7 may be just a footnote to your audience. If you're meeting with your boss, executive management, or a potential investor, you're one of a dozen—if not a hundred—projects, opportunities, or problems that have their mindshare that hour, day, or week. They don't live in your world, and they never will. So, don't take anything for granted. Before you declare victory and move on to the next task, make sure that you have actually connected your audience with the vision that you're working so hard to achieve.

Help them embrace it and make it their own.

FIND YOUR HOOK TO CAPTURE ATTENTION FROM THE START

Your opening frame is critical.

You have maybe five minutes to get 90 percent of the room on your side.

While you could begin with something provocative and challenging, as we discussed earlier, this is likely to put people on the defensive and leave a lot of broken glass.

People are increasingly experiencing information overload and attention deficit. If you start with the data, they will likely question the numbers or struggle to empathize, identify, or relate.

You have just a few precious minutes to capture your audience's attention and establish relevance. How can you convince them to care about what your message?

Remind them of what's possible.

Start with YES! Capture the imagination, get people leaning in, excited, and intrigued.

To quote Victor Hugo, "There is nothing like a dream to create the future." Be a messenger from the future. Bring the good news.

Share your excitement about what you see. Show your audience how change equals possibility.

Present a compelling context for change that is a generally accepted truth. You want people to say, *Wow, I knew there was something going on. But I didn't realize it had come this far. I've been waiting for this moment.* Remember we're aiming for 90 percent. And because you have such limited time, keep your context clear and simple. The destination should be a visible point in the distance, not a blurry mess.

It's your job to show people what is possible now. Use this change in the world—the things that weren't around 5 or 10 years ago, such as ridesharing apps or blockchain—that may legitimize and validate the premise of your idea. Maybe there's been a big technological breakthrough that has changed everything, such as advances in autonomous vehicles. Or the economics have come down so you can do now what five years ago was 100x or 1,000x the cost. Or cultural values have shifted in a way that people are ready for something that only a few years ago seemed outside the mainstream. Twenty years ago, organic produce was just for hippies. Now, grandmothers in Texas are eating tofu. Gay marriage was a taboo topic a generation ago, simply off-limits from mainstream political discourse. Until activists changed the story from one about human rights to one about love. Love is a hard story to stand in the way of.

A great story transports your audience from where they are now to a point in the future where they want to go. Your story should be so engaging, so inspiring, so enticing that you won't have to push people to join you. They'll be drawn to your vision of the future. Do this by focusing on the meta story—the big picture.

Story is like GPS in your car—both a location device and a transportation vehicle.

As a location device, its job is to help people locate themselves. Where do they belong? Is this a story they identify with as their own? As a transportation vehicle, a story takes us places. The question is, where is it going, and do we want to go there? What's the promise of the destination? Do you have a story worth telling? Or a pizza with nothing on it?

Done effectively, you can lead your audience from the impossible to the inevitable. From the predictability of the status quo to the payoff of an emergent future.

NAME THE CHANGE

Change is the only constant. A story is, by definition, about change. The very reason that "communicating the new" is so challenging can also be your saving grace. Change is what makes a story. No change, no story. The reason we keep paying attention to a story is that it keeps changing. We want to know where it's going. Our interest is engaged, stimulated, and held as we follow the tension and the arc of the narrative. In a good story, we're invested in the characters and the situation. We want to know: how does the story end? And then, like after a good cliffhanger, what happened?

Thankfully, there are lots of changes for you to talk about. Whatever is most relevant to your work and business at hand. Consider these examples:

- Changes in how we diagnose illness and treat cancer
- Changes in how we buy our food and what we eat
- Changes in how we build community and find others like us
- Changes in how we work, communicate, and get stuff done
- Changes in how we date and find our life mate
- Changes in how we manage our finances and plan for the future
- Changes in how we develop software, interfaces, or interactions

- Changes in how our customers tell stories and interact with our brands
- Changes in how we buy things and choose what we really want

What are some changes affecting *your* industry?

Lucky for you, it doesn't take much to identify change these days. Change is the new normal. Disruption is predicated on the assumption of constant, massive, overwhelming change. Which means, amid all that confusion and anticipation, change is redefining one or more aspects of how things used to be done. It's creating new paradigms—new ways of looking at the world.

Your job is to narrate the change. But the trick is to be an evangelist for it. What is the good news about this change? What will draw people to it? Why should someone want to embrace it? In other words, what's in it for them? So often we get caught in describing change as a looming threat (cortisol) instead of describing change as a breakthrough opportunity around something we share in common (oxytocin). Remember you're not pushing a PhD thesis here. Present a positive, affirmative statement of what's possible now that wasn't before and how this helps make the case for whatever it is that you are proposing.

How you frame this will in great part determine how people react to it—and whether or not you will succeed. Use language and rhetoric to strengthen your message.

CONVERGENCE OF FORCES

The currents of change are always flowing.

If you work in Silicon Valley, you might have a better sense of the exponential futures in front of us. We're currently experiencing radical leaps in technology in areas such as artificial intelligence, augmented reality, big data, the internet of things, blockchain, and so much more. Only 30 years ago, Tim Berners-Lee created the first version of the World Wide Web. Today, it's ubiquitous. It pervades our lives. Our organizations. It connects us.

Twenty-first-century companies face compressed technology cycles, which create the need for continuous innovation. At the same time, cultural changes are redefining social behaviors— digital identity, privacy, and emotional self-care habits, among others. Similarly, large established companies in traditional industries might be having a hard time anticipating how much technology is going to transform their incumbent business models. Take the legal profession as an example. Offshoring of talent, along with AI, is increasingly dropping the bottom out of their economic model. Some of these changes are easy to see. Others we are prone to overlook.

An effective storyteller takes the convergence of forces— technological, economic, and cultural—and puts them into context for their audience.

- **Technological forces:** hardware, software, interfaces, surfaces, bandwidth, etc.

- **Economic forces:** lower costs, greater availability, changes in supply/demand, etc.

- **Cultural forces:** new social values, emergent trends, redefinition of norms, etc.

You can explore these forces further in Oren Klaff's book *Pitch Anything*.

Investors love a pitch that makes a case for a convergence of forces. I recently worked with the CEO of a venture-backed startup in the midst of raising their Series E. As part of their pitch to private equity investors, they talked about the convergence of

"Human beings all change.
Not what they are but who
they are. We have the power
to change what we do
with our life and turn it into
our destiny."

———

ELIE WIESEL

forces that supports peer-to-peer marketplaces as the future of commerce. Investors loved this premise of where the world is going and how this matched their investment thesis. That this startup is the natural fit to fulfill that inevitable future becomes a foregone conclusion. That's the power you harness when you describe where the future is headed.

In the case of a psychological testing company, an executive team repeatedly considers the potential disruptions ahead and their pace of digital transformation. It's what Robert Tercek describes in his book *Vaporized* as an "unstoppable force," how digital products are eating the world. Anything print or analog will eventually become vaporized by the inevitability of digital transformation. This is how the "Venmo curve" became a rallying cry among the leadership team of this company.

If you're 20 or 30 years old, odds are you use Venmo all the time to transfer money between friends. If you're in your 40s or 50s, you've maybe used it on occasion. And if you're in your 60s or 70s, odds are you're thinking, *What's Venmo?* Venmo is a new category of smartphone app that allows for peer-to-peer financial transactions without any fees. The adoption of Venmo is a direct reflection of demographics. It serves as a metaphor for how digital transformation is becoming an absolute requirement for old-school protected industries.

If most of your customers or users are Baby Boomers, you still have some time to transition from analog to digital. As Millennials become the dominant generation in the workplace, they'll expect the same ease of use and instant gratification provided by Venmo, Amazon, and Netflix. No matter what industry you are in, it's not a question of *if* but of *when*. It's an inevitable future. So, the question is, how does our leadership team prepare and build for that world? The good news? They have at least 5 to 10 years to align with this inevitable future.

In the case of a supply chain consulting company, the disruptive forces include the Amazon effect, transportation costs, and omni-channel convergence. This means that every consumer packaged-goods company and industrial manufacturer they work with are facing similar trends:

1   The Amazon effect means consumers now expect two-day free shipping on everything, whether it's a small book or a 2,000-pound piece of machinery.

2   Transportation costs are one of the biggest drags on growth as companies face a rising cost of trucking due to gasoline prices and greater demand than supply of truckers in states like California.

3   Omnichannel convergence requires a supply chain solution that provides visibility on both direct-to-consumer and direct-to-store inventory needs.

When the sales team of this supply chain company describes this convergence of forces to a prospective client, they immediately establish resonance and rapport.

In the case of craft chocolate, you've got an epic and exciting convergence similar to how beer, wine, coffee, and cheese have grown into specialty food categories with a premium paid for quality and provenance. Except in this case, *everyone* loves chocolate. Young and old. Rich and poor. Craft chocolate is an affordable luxury and healthy indulgence, a sensuously flavorful reward and re-energizer. The convergence of forces include:

1   Chocolate is a scientifically proven superfood and mood enhancer

2   The relatively accessible price point of "upgraded" chocolate at $10–20/bar

3   The explosion of craft chocolate-makers (600-plus worldwide) and availability of heirloom cacao with fine flavor tasting notes

All of these convergences make chocolate an exciting and growing food category, perfect for our health-conscious times.

To survive and thrive, you need to read the tea leaves better or faster than others. You also need to describe how you're uniquely poised to take advantage of the coming change in a way others can't or won't be. Behind every billion-dollar unicorn startup was a convergence of forces that redefined the game in its specific industry. That created a new opportunity ripe to be exploited. That changed everything. So much is possible today that wasn't possible even just 5 or 10 years ago. Much less 5 to 10 years into the future. Many limitations we have today will be gone tomorrow. Take a look at the environment in which you're doing business. What are the convergence of forces? How do these changes equal possibility? How will they generate even more new possibilities?

RETHINKING CHANGE AS A "BURNING PLATFORM"

There is a popular catchphrase in the field of change management. According to the experts, a change initiative needs a *burning platform* to motivate people. Otherwise, people won't change, the organization won't change, and yet another change initiative will fail.

The idea of a burning platform is reflected in this memo that former Nokia CEO Stephen Elop sent out to his employees in 2011 when Apple's iPhone and Google's Android phone were eating Nokia's lunch. Nokia—once the most-successful mobile

Exercise: Describe the Convergence of Forces

Okay, it's your turn. Take a moment to assess the convergence of forces—
technological, economic, and cultural—at work in your business and put
them into context for your audience. Make a list of at least three items
for each of the three forces and use them to tell your *Undeniable Story.*

Technological forces (such as hardware and software)

1 _____

2 _____

3 _____

Economic forces (such as lower costs and greater availability)

1 _____

2 _____

3 _____

Cultural forces (such as new social values and emergent trends)

1 _____

2 _____

3 _____

phone company in the world—had lost its way. Here's the story of the burning platform as Elop told it:

> There is a story about a man who was working on an oil platform in the North Sea. He woke up one night from a loud explosion, which suddenly set his entire oil platform on fire. In mere moments, he was surrounded by flames. Through the smoke and heat, he barely made his way out of the chaos to the platform's edge. When he looked down over the edge, all he could see were the dark, cold, foreboding Atlantic waters.
>
> As the fire approached him, the man had mere seconds to react. He could stand on the platform and inevitably be consumed by the burning flames. Or he could plunge 30 meters in to the freezing waters. The man was standing upon a "burning platform," and he needed to make a choice.
>
> He decided to jump. It was unexpected. In ordinary circumstances, the man would never consider plunging into icy waters. But these were not ordinary times—his platform was on fire. The man survived the fall and the waters. After he was rescued, he noted that a "burning platform" caused a radical change in his behavior. We too are standing on a "burning platform," and we must decide how we are going to change our behavior.[6]

I'm curious: how do you feel when you read a story like that? Is it motivating? Or demoralizing?

The metaphor of the burning platform maybe isn't quite the right message. If you stay, you're going to die. And if you jump, you're still probably going to die. Hey, maybe we'll beat the odds like Louis Zamperini, the famous World War II veteran, who survived 46 days adrift at sea, only to then endure a Japanese prison camp where he was tortured repeatedly. His incredible story was later retold in the international bestselling book and movie *Unbroken*. Which is an absolutely wonderful story. But is that kind of future the one you want to sell to your people? And we wonder why more than 70 percent of change management initiatives fail. Hopefully you appreciate the power of avoiding cortisol—fight/flight/freeze—as a motivational driver. We have to give people more confidence in the future than just a leap of faith, on a wing and a prayer.

Whenever you introduce a New Story, you bring into focus and contrast the Old Story. The best kinds of New Stories don't reject the Old Stories but rather demonstrate a natural evolution. A contrast frame between the Old Story and New Story is a powerful way to draw out distinctions and help people to understand the paradigm shift.

Remember that outsiders—consultants, advisors, etc.—often have more credibility than do insiders. Harvard Business School professor Clayton Christensen tells a story about a fast-food chain that wanted to sell more milkshakes. They obsessed over the qualities of the shake. Should it have more flavor? Should it be thicker? Should it contain more syrup? Less? This approach did not lead them to any great insights.

So, the fast-food chain hired a pair of consultants to take a look at the problem. They went through all the data and discovered something surprising. A large number of milkshakes were purchased during the morning hours in the drive-thru—for breakfast. For these customers, milkshakes had a *job to be done*. Tide them over until lunch on the morning commute. A bagel is full of crumbs, while a banana leaves behind a stinky peel. A milkshake, on the other hand, is easy to drink while driving, and its thickness means it lasts awhile. It will fill you up without ruining your appetite for lunch. So what is the *job to be done* that was driving disproportionate milkshake sales before 9 a.m.? A milkshake occupies a customer's right hand on their morning commute to work.

Exercise: Old Story/New Story

Frame the change in contrast of then and now. In this exercise, you'll have a chance to practice.

Take a piece of paper, and in landscape orientation, create two columns with a line down the middle. Label the left column "Old Story" and the right column "New Story." In the left column, describe the Old Story based on a series of keywords, phrases, values, and mindsets. And in the right-hand column, do the same, trying to match the Old Story words to their New Story equivalents.

The example that follows is built around a company that has completely disrupted the hospitality industry: Airbnb. Consider how Airbnb has created a New Story, with a product so compelling that it has garnered a $38 billion valuation and a market cap that outpaces Marriott or Hilton. Despite the fact that Airbnb doesn't even own real estate. That's an *Undeniable Story* in action.

OLD STORY	NEW STORY
Hotel beige	Homey feeling
Standardized culture	Soul of a city
Transactional	Relational
Monopoly pricing	Democratized pricing
Be restrained	Belong anywhere

What's your Old Story and what's your New Story? Follow the example above to define your key elements. Then use them as ingredients when you craft your own *Undeniable Story*.

The fast-food chain's Old Story was overtaken by a New Story. Milkshakes aren't just dessert anymore. Milkshakes are the perfect morning meal.

How would your Old Stories change if they were replaced with New Stories? What insights would you gain as a result?

STORYTELLING TIPS AND TRICKS

To succeed in your high-stakes presentation, you have to show your audience the context for change. Help them embrace the inevitability of the future that you're describing and the opportunities that come with being out in front of the change. Do this well, and your vision is undeniable. Here are four cautionary reminders as you put this storytelling strategy into practice.

- **Pick the right battles to fight.** Use your energy intelligently. It's rarely wise to open with something contentious, controversial, or debatable. Instead, present a compelling context for change that is a generally accepted truth. Focus on what everybody wants. What will create a natural momentum of *yes*? In the next chapter, I'll talk about how to humanize your big idea.

- **Focus on what's right instead of on what's wrong.** Why put people into a fight/flight/freeze (cortisol) state? You want the context for change to be aspirational, filled with an opportunity statement that is exciting. Otherwise, you risk your audience taking your message personally and interpreting that you are suggesting they are wrong, bad, or stupid. Putting your audience on the defensive is not a winning persuasive proposition.

- **Avoid the seven-layer burrito.** It may sound delicious, until you're about three bites in and your stomach starts to turn.

Don't make your opening so complex that it gives your audience indigestion. Focus on a clear premise. What is the most dramatic and compelling way that the world is changing? Explain it in a way that makes what you're doing more obvious than ever before. It's ideally a single idea, with at most two or three supporting points.

- **Don't get ahead of the story.** Remember you live and breathe what you're working on. Which means you might already be in Chapter 9 of the story, when most of your audience is back in Chapter 2 or 3. Which is why you want to frame the context properly, and invite the audience to come along the journey with you. What might be blatantly obvious to you is what everyone most wants or needs to know. Take the time to slow down. Odds are people need to be reminded of the bigger picture, even if it seems rather self-evident to you.

In this chapter, we explored how critical it is for others to see what you see, in order for them to embrace your story and make it their own. We considered how to find the right hook for your story. One that captures your audience's attention right away. We saw how change creates story and that your job is to narrate the change. We looked at the convergence of three forces and how to put them in context for your audience. And why you should reconsider the idea of change as a burning platform.

Again, keep in mind that this is not a PhD thesis. You will have ample opportunity later in your *Undeniable Story* to circle back to your opening premise and further color the convergent trends.

Now that we've established the context for change, let's next consider how to inject emotion into your story.

"Everyone is the
hero of their own story.
Do your best not
to be the villain in
someone else's."

WIL WHEATON

5

Step 2: Feel It— The Emotional Dilemma

IN THIS CHAPTER

- **Making your character the hero**

- **Giving your character a conflict**

- **Conflict beyond hero/victim/villain**

- **How to craft a customer avatar**

- **A character study in 30 days**

IT'S NOT EASY to sell the future when your customers are in a panic about it. Yet this was the case for a Silicon Valley startup in the customer support category.

What if you could access the wisdom of those closest to your product—that is, your power users—as part of the customer support experience? As a bridge between the online FAQ that's always out of date and the customer service rep on the phone halfway around the world who's reading from a script and doesn't know your product.

Fresh off raising $10 million in their Series A, this company needed to pivot from their Investor Story to the Client Story. While venture capital was enamored with the 10-year vision (AI, big data, and the future of work), their B2B enterprise clients were more indexed to the challenges on the immediate horizon. Think about it: if you're the VP of customer support inside a big company, your day-to-day reality is a *giant pile of suck*. You're expected to manage higher-ticket volumes, at a lower cost, without compromising on customer happiness. And here comes "attack of the killer chatbots" and artificial intelligence with the promise to transform your business. It's a little too much risk for most enterprise leaders. They know they need to embrace AI, yet they're afraid of all the things that can and do go wrong.

Telling this complex story became of critical importance to this startup's growth. It allowed them to have a new kind of sales conversation rooted in nuanced understanding of the challenges their clients faced. Their breakthrough message? "How to scale empathy in the age of automation." It was a powerful way to humanize their work and brand a new category—CX automation—focused on the customer experience. Built through a community-powered AI engine, power users actually train and teach the algorithms to create a low-friction, high-impact meaningful interaction.

That's the thing with your big-picture story—you have to balance the *zoom out* with the *zoom in*. If the first step in convincing your audience is telling the meta story, the second step is telling the micro story. You've framed the context for your audience, but they're primed for more. Now you need to draw them into the *emotional* content. When you do that successfully, you'll create raving fans—true believers in your *Undeniable Story*.

There's just one thing: emotion is one of the hardest things to work with in business (and life).

We tend to avoid it, squash it—or self-indulge in it. The extremes.

Instead of living at the extremes of emotion, we must learn how to work with it. It's a signal for finding where the real story is. Emotion is not the essence of your message, emotion colors and gives meaning to it. Infuses it with life.

Storytelling expert Lisa Cron sums it up like this:

> Feeling is a reaction; our feelings let us know what matters to us, and our thoughts have no choice but to follow. Facts that don't affect us—either directly or because we can't imagine how the facts affect someone else—don't matter to us. And that explains why one personalized story has infinitely more impact than an impersonal generalization, even though the scope of the generalization is a thousand times greater.[7]

How do you get emotion into your story? Every story is about the characters who inhabit it, and all dramatic tension comes from the desires and dilemmas of those characters. In this chapter, you'll learn how to pick and describe a character central to the story, with a set of needs that aren't easily met or resolved. This means we're going to have to get up close and personal. We'll draw an intimate portrait so we can see the story take shape in clear and moving terms.

If you're the parent of a child with special needs, odds are that life isn't easy. You've probably struggled to understand how to best meet your child's needs. Early on, you felt that something wasn't quite right and you sought out help. Then, if and when a diagnosis was made, you needed to navigate a complex and fragmented bureaucracy of support to get help for your child. As you started to interact with school officials, clinical psychologists, and other helping professionals, you found yourself conflicted. On one hand, you wanted to know what was happening with your child. On the other hand, you were afraid of a diagnosis or limiting label.

That's the challenge that practitioners face when asked to assess a child. They have 120 minutes over 30 days to determine what is going on. Their report may impact at least the next 10 years, if not the rest, of this child's life—for good and for bad. And these practitioners not only face pressure from parents but must manage complex compliance and administrative requirements in the conduct of their work. This is the emotional landscape at the heart of this story. Most psychological testing companies think they just create tests. In reality, they're developing and delivering solutions against this emotional backdrop. Therein lies the future of this business and the whitespace for innovation. Solve against unmet emotional needs by painting a more intimate portrait of the realities on the ground.

Emotion is the fuel of every story. It's what propels the action forward. You need to get your audience to care, to feel invested in the outcome. Which means we need to zero in on the characters at the center of your story. Who they are, what motivates them, and what obstacles they face.

Who are the characters in your story?

What are their desires and dilemmas?

What will they do or give in order to reach their goal?

Each of us brings our own emotions into everything we do, both in our work and in our personal lives. These feelings serve as filters—gatekeepers for our perception of the world around us. They determine to a great degree whether or not we accept, much less embrace, what someone tells us.

Empathy flows both ways—it's not a top-down or one-way experience. You can create that flow by empathizing with your audience first. To get your audience invested in the outcome, they must take it on as their own story and put themselves inside it. Essentially, they must empathize with the characters and invest in the narrative emotionally to accept it as their own.

MAKE YOUR CUSTOMER THE HERO

When in doubt, make your customer the hero of the story.

For many organizations, determining who your customer or user is can be difficult. This is even more challenging when you consider all the different stakeholders that you need to influence. How do you decide who to put at the center of the story? Make it the most relatable character.

In the technology industry, there is a common habit of making the product or the brand the hero of the story, instead of a person. When you present a product as hero, you're focused on its amazing and remarkable features and benefits. Computers are common victims of this practice—highlighting faster processors, more RAM, and larger, hard (and now solid state) drives. This practice can create a muddy focal point, resulting in stories that are far too self-congratulatory or more technical in detail than the average consumer can handle.

Instead, the focus should be on the *user* of that product. What is that person trying to accomplish? What are the *jobs to be done*? What do they aspire to create or achieve through the use of this product? What are the frustrating obstacles that they keep coming up against? Where do they feel pain? How will this new thing help the user accomplish more and leap over the obstacles in their path?

When you're searching for the right kind of person to turn into a hero, the best candidate is that individual whose life you have the greatest potential to impact. Your most direct *sphere of influence*. Remember, this person will serve as a persona for thousands if not millions of others. People who share the same desires and challenges, or are somewhat similar or related to them. When figuring out who you put at the center of the story, think about the people within your sphere of influence.

Here's another example.

An executive team was tasked with building the next-generation campus of their Silicon Valley HQ. They were put in charge of a multi-billion-dollar investment, focused on the future of work.

At first, they made the company's end consumers (customers) the hero of the story. The logic was that by creating a better campus that would propel innovation and help their business recruit top-tier talent, they would provide life-changing positive health outcomes for consumers. That was all well and good, but there was just one problem: this top executive and their 200-person facilities organization didn't actually have any control or influence

"Our research has shown that you will never fully engage an audience—and you need to fully engage them in order to influence them—unless you involve them at an emotional level. Stories do that."

KENDALL HAVEN

on the end consumer of the company's products. What *did* they have influence over? The lives of 20,000 employees and partners who worked at and visited the corporate campus every day. Historically, the employee experience was owned by HR, corporate affairs, and even IT. Not the facilities organization. They needed a story big enough to co-create with and engage these other internal stakeholders.

When this executive changed the focus and put the company's *employees* at the center of the story, their ability to influence dramatically rose. In the case of this team's narrative, these were the characters they had the greatest ability to impact. And the result? The full $2 billion budget they requested and more. The entire company rallied around their vision for the future of the campus, despite all that comes with massive renovations, disruption of core infrastructure, and nonstop construction, road detours, and inconveniences.

Remember the human brain doesn't pay attention to or care about your story unless we're able to say, *That sounds or looks like me.*

This is true whether the characters are humans or animals or robots or whatever they may be. We need to belong in the story. To identify with the character's needs and motivations.

Who is the character of your story? Who will your audience most relate to and feel empathy for? If you're struggling to decide who to put at the center of your story, start with your customer or user. Here are a few examples.

- Apple's famous "Get a Mac" campaign presents two contrasting characters ("Hello, I'm a Mac. And I'm a PC")—the Mac user as a cool creative and the PC user as a boring square.

- Retailer REI understands their audience. On Black Friday, the busiest shopping day of the year, they close their stores, encouraging consumers to #OptOutside, instead of opting into the ritual of consumerism.

- Old Spice had lost its relevance, until they reimagined a brand voice and personality designed for women through their "The Man Your Man Could Smell Like" campaign.

GIVE YOUR CHARACTER A CONFLICT

As much as we may want to avoid conflict in our own lives, we love stories of characters who are in conflict. David versus Goliath. Dorothy versus the Wicked Witch of the West. Elon Musk versus short sellers of Tesla stock. Conflict sparks our feelings and emotions, and it gives stories suspense, texture, and interest. To make your character—and your story—compelling, you need to have some form of conflict.

"Difficulties are meant to rouse, not discourage. The human spirit is to grow strong by conflict."

WILLIAM ELLERY CHANNING

Bill Grundfest, Golden Globe-winning writer and founder of the legendary Comedy Cellar, once explained to me that, in Hollywood, there's a basic screenwriting formula: "Who wants what? What gets in their way?"

Every TV show is built on the same fundamental emotional premise. In other words, your character has to have a desire for someone or something (Who wants what?) and has to face an obstacle or dilemma (What gets in their way?). It doesn't matter what genre we're talking about or what medium. This basic story truth applies universally.

Let's explore, for example, the timeless themes of power and integrity. That's the story of *The Sopranos*, an HBO episodic drama full of crime and violence. Tony Soprano (played by James Gandolfini) is a mob boss who is trying to build and hold onto his power. Every episode explores Tony's battle for power and, over time, the growing existential struggle he faces about the costs of gaining and maintaining power and the meaning of life.

That's equally the story of *Veep*, an HBO episodic comedy. In this case, Selina Meyer (played by Julia Louis-Dreyfus) is a power-hungry politician on a constant quest for more power. Every episode explores her quest for power, and the mishaps that occur when vanity and ego get in the way.

These two television shows inhabit very different genres (one is a drama and one is a comedy), but they explore the same universal premises—power and integrity. Each succeeds in its own way.

So, what makes for an interesting character? How do you bring their story to life? You start with a central character—someone who wants something, yet something else gets in the way. That desire versus dilemma is what propels all great timeless stories. The story is about the journey the character goes on to get what they want. What are they willing to do, pay, give up, sacrifice, change, in the process?

Think about your favorite film, book, or television character for a moment. Harry Potter from *Harry Potter and the Philosopher's Stone*. Ellen Ripley from *Alien*. Walter White from *Breaking Bad*.

Harry Potter is an orphan child who lives in the cupboard underneath the stairs of his maternal aunt's home in England. He's a natural-born wizard but doesn't know this yet. He's young, innocent, and awkward. He's the chosen one but will only discover this as time goes on and fate reveals itself. He's an easy character to relate to, since most of us at some point have felt like a misfit who doesn't belong.

Ellen Ripley is a warrant officer on the spaceship *Nostromo*, returning to Earth from the planet Thedus sometime in the near future. An alien creature boards the spaceship and kills all the members of the crew except for her. Ellen is tough, tenacious, independent. She's not an accessory for the male members of the crew or inferior to them in any way. Ellen is fully their equal. And, ultimately, she defeats the deadly alien. She's the strong woman that we've all been waiting for. In the process, she defies gender stereotypes and shows what an empowered female hero can look like.

Walter White is the complex lead character of the television series *Breaking Bad*. He's a chemistry teacher who can't pay the bills. He has a son with special needs, a marriage that's on the rocks, and terminal cancer. This propels him on a wild adventure into cooking methamphetamine and taking on powerful drug kingpins, both north and south of the Mexican border. He's an anti-hero, yet we find ourselves cheering for him despite the bad choices he often makes.

The best, timeless characters are complex. While they face external conflicts in the world around them, it's the journey through their *internal* conflicts that is the real underlying story. This is a key nuance to keep in mind when building out Step 2: Feel It for your *Undeniable Story*.

"I think the best stories always end up being about the people rather than the event, which is to say character-driven."

———

STEPHEN KING

REDEFINING CONFLICT:
AVOIDING HERO, VICTIM, VILLAIN

Classical storytelling was built for the age of certainty. It often frames ideas in an adversarial or oppositional way. There's the problem, here's the solution.

Us versus them.

Right versus wrong.

Winners versus losers.

In this age of disruption, with worldviews and value systems colliding, strict adversarial opposition doesn't work like it used to. Your audience often has a different cosmology or codex of rules for what is possible/impossible, acceptable/unacceptable, real/ unreal. The content of your disruptive vision challenges the very boundaries of those dualities. We want stories that go beyond a zero-sum game.

This is a hard habit to break. We've spent the last 10,000-plus years telling stories about *us versus them*. In stories, we're used to thinking of the good guy and the bad guy, the hero and the villain. We naturally vilify the "other," the "stranger," that which is different.

Why does that long-standing model pose a problem for disruptive storytellers? Because we no longer exist in our isolated, removed, clear-cut tribes. With social media and communications technology, a new global culture is emerging, where we are all more interconnected (and interdependent than ever before). This can be bewildering as the safety and comfort of our smaller worlds and stories come into direct conflict with the stories of another tribal identity. It makes for quite the evolutionary moment. It's why a new kind of storytelling holds so much promise.

Psychologist Stephen Karpman conducted a fascinating bit of research on this dynamic. It's summarized in a diagram called the Karpman Drama Triangle.[8] According to Karpman, the emotional reversals that constitute drama can be summarized in just three roles: persecutor, rescuer, and victim. The hero or heroine of any dramatic story switches from role to role depending on the action that is occurring at any given time. According to Karpman, there is no drama if there is no switch in roles.

The Karpman Drama Triangle looks like this:

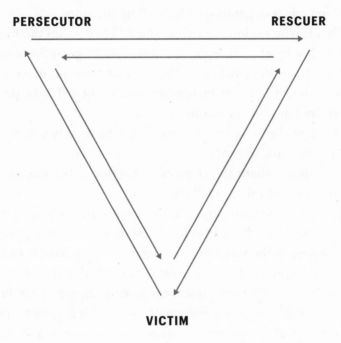

Let's consider our own adaptation of this model: hero, victim, villain. In classical storytelling, the moment you have a hero, you need a victim and villain. Equally if you have a victim, you need a hero and villain. Without Lord Voldemort, the dark wizard, or the wizarding world to save, could Harry Potter truly become the hero we adore?

One cautionary note. One person's hero may be another's villain. Consider the case of Julian Assange, founder of WikiLeaks. Some, like the ACLU, cast him as a hero for First Amendment rights and journalistic transparency. Others, like the U.S. government, cast him as a villain for revealing highly classified secrets, putting national security at risk. What do *you* think? Might both stories be true? Characters are complex. Perhaps Assange started out as a hero, then crossed the line to villain? Or perhaps he started out as a villain, then crossed the line to hero? It depends who you ask. It depends on who's telling the story.

This is why we love stories so much. They reveal the human experience in all its complexity. And it works great for film, TV, and literature. But what about the real world, the business world, as we interact with an increasing number of different people, tribes, institutions, and nation-states?

If you're the hero, that's great—but who exactly wants to be the victim or the villain?

And that's where the story of disruption gets more complicated than classical storytelling.

Too often, someone in our audience of stakeholders is cast as the victim or the villain. In many cases, unconsciously so. Anyone who stands in the way of the change, or is responsible or complicit in the problem, is cast as the villain. That's a surefire recipe to get those people to exit out of the story or trigger a fight/flight/freeze (cortisol) response in them. If you're having a problem with your story feeling lost in translation, odds are that you've unconsciously cast one of your stakeholders as the victim or the villain (and they would rather not inhabit either role).

The Karpman Drama Triangle perhaps reflects more of our past as a storytelling species than the future we are moving into. Especially if you are trying to shift a paradigm or bring forward innovation in your respective industry or organization. When it comes to disruption, you have to go beyond the hero/victim/villain story. Instead, focus on the internal conflicts the hero faces, the creative tension between desire and dilemma, what they want and what gets in their way. Doing that builds empathy, which has the power to transcend and overcome any differences that separate us, by reinforcing how we are similar. Help us find and connect to our shared humanity.

Watch my bonus video on hero/victim/villain stories, go to getstoried.com/worldchanging.

HOW TO CRAFT A RELATABLE AVATAR

In our storytelling workshops, participants do a variety of exercises to unpack the desire and emotional dilemma at the heart of their narratives. Describing an internal conflict with true empathy for what your character faces is the real secret to cracking the code for an *Undeniable Story*. One of the most popular exercises we do is creating a persona. Those of you schooled in design-thinking tools like Empathy Mapping or Persona Development may be familiar with the basic outlines of this exercise.

The big gap that often emerges in traditional personas and avatars is the over-rationalization of a character's emotional life. We paint the picture of an individual and their needs, desires, and challenges in a way that provides the self-delusion that we know what's really going on.

Humans are rational beings. And make rational choices.

Not exactly. That is a false belief, a problem/solution mindset.

In reality, humans are complex creatures—anything but linear and predictable. We are full of contradictions and paradoxes. Tony Soprano, Ellen Ripley, and Walter White are tremendously complex people—and heroes. While we may not always agree with the decisions they make, they are relatable because of their foibles and paradoxes. We feel empathy for them and for their lot in life.

Your emotional truth must connect with your audience's emotional truth. If you have a hard time doing a character study, this signals that you are not close enough to your story. You need to roll up your sleeves and get dirty. You can do that through focus groups, interviews, user surveys, ethnographic research, listening tours, or other learning journeys.

A CHARACTER STUDY IN 30 DAYS

While you might be able to complete your character study (see exercise on the next page) within a few hours, 30 days is a better timeline to work with. You don't want to rush it. This is definitely a case where the quality of results is more important than quantity or speed.

STORYTELLING TIPS AND TRICKS

Of course, there are many ways to go wrong as you develop your main character. Here are some tips that will help you stay on the right course.

Choose the right hero. Make sure you're casting a hero that you have the ability to influence and impact with your product, service, or solution. Don't try to solve for something outside your direct sphere of control. That's a recipe for failure.

Describe your character in aspirational terms. It's easy when doing a character study to let your frustrations with a character seep in. In other words, you may have a complicated relationship with this character (aka customer, user, member, etc.). Perhaps they haven't always embraced your company's role in wanting to

Exercise: Create a Character Study

Ask these questions to craft your character study:

- Define the key characters in your story.
- Pick the top three to five. Who's the hero or protagonist?
- From whose vantage point should you tell the story?
- What do they want, what gets in the way?
- What is their desire and what is their dilemma?
- How do they see themselves? How does the world see them?
- What assumptions can you test and validate about your character?
- What research could you do to get closer to your character?

Name:

Age:

Profession:

Matrix:

Desire:

Dilemma:

Inner Perceptions:

External Perceptions:

"I'm not that interested in recreating reality. I'm interested in recreating an emotional truth."

———

GUILLERMO DEL TORO

serve and make a difference. Or maybe they are skeptical of your brand. Avoid the temptation to describe them in condescending or pejorative terms. Make it a love story! Even if they are difficult, what are their redeeming or endearing qualities? Don't make your characters wrong for wanting what they want.

Go beyond victims and villains. If you truly want to move the world, you need a message that transcends what separates us. The more your narrative is built on adversarial, oppositional, or divisive framing, the more you will get stuck in the very story you are trying to transcend. It's a rhetorical trap and a self-fulfilling prophecy. Avoid it or pay the price of what is very likely unnecessary bloodshed and endless battle.

Avoid false resolution. The blind spot of Empathy Mapping and typical advertising/marketing personas is the presentation of an over-rationalized diagnosis and solution. Unless you're selling toothpaste or diapers, your issue is complicated. Honor the paradox that your character faces, as it will make for a more real and interesting story. Also, if you solve the problem too early, where's the story going to go next? There is nowhere to go after "The End." So, try to avoid a premature conclusion.

In this chapter, we saw the awesome power of making your customer the hero. We also learned how putting your character in conflict makes them more compelling. More interesting. More real. We explored the Karpman Drama Triangle and how to craft a relatable avatar. Finally, I showed you a quick-and-easy way to create a character study.

As you can see, emotion is a key ingredient in any compelling story. Combined with the context for change, you're two-thirds of the way to crafting your *Undeniable Story* and multiplying your outcomes. What's missing is the third key ingredient: the evidence of truth. That's the subject of the next chapter.

"Stories are,
just maybe, data
with a soul."

BRENÉ BROWN

6

Step 3: Believe It— The Evidence of Truth

IN THIS CHAPTER

- **Truth be told**

- **Using data to support your promise**

- **15 sources of evidence**

- **Troubleshooting truth**

SUMMER VACATION HAD sputtered to a stop, and it was my first day back to school. I looked forward to the second grade with a mix of trepidation and anticipation. Catching up with old friends. Meeting some new ones.

But first my new teacher had a special announcement to make. She carefully unfolded a letter she had received from Zoo de Servion, a wild animal refuge. She began to read...

Dear Madame Chameau and the second grade at École du Tombay—
You have been carefully selected to assist us in a special task. Our zoo will be undergoing massive renovations this year. And in support of the welfare of our animals during this time, we are asking local families to help room and board some of our animals during the transition. Your classroom has been chosen for this special honor.

The classroom erupted with shrieks of excitement. We immediately started debating which animals each of us would get to bring home. Sophie rode horses, so her assignment was obvious. Nicholas had a fascination with frogs, so we all knew what he would ask for. Vincent always wanted a pet raccoon, so that was his choice.

Me? I instantly knew. I'd be bringing home a 15-foot-long boa constrictor snake from the Amazon jungle. I loved snakes as a kid. But my mother had a mortal fear of them. This was one pet forbidden from our home.

You can imagine the dinnertime drama as I explained to my family what had happened on my first day of school, and that we would be boarding a boa constrictor for the entire school year ahead. My mother was understandably very eager to get to the bottom of this tale. She assured me that the next morning she would march into school to talk with my teacher.

NO!! I was so embarrassed and afraid of losing my snake that I threw an epic tantrum. One for the ages. I didn't want my mother to leave the house. I even tried to throw her car keys down a storm drain. This story remains a legend in my family, and it will likely live on well after I am gone.

I share it with you to illustrate the power of our brain on story.

As a kid, I just knew this story was *real*. Our teacher, a trusted authority figure, had read us a letter from Zoo de Servion, the local animal refuge. Another trusted authority. And it said that we would be spending the next several months on this important assignment. I felt special. Chosen. Blessed. Because one of my wildest dreams was about to come true.

Except it wasn't. Of course, our teacher apologized profusely to my mom and other parents after she received a dozen concerned phone calls the next day. The letter wasn't real. The zoo had not made this remarkable offer. Our teacher explained that she was just trying to get us kids excited and in a receptive mindset to study the animal kingdom that school year.

Have you ever experienced a story that you later found out to be false? How did it make you feel? What did you think about the person or company that told you the story? Did you trust them afterward?

When you're doing something that's never been done before, you're faced with a particularly difficult challenge. You're selling people on something that doesn't exist yet, or at least not fully. It's a *potential* future. And, as we've seen, if your audience can't see and feel that potential future, how will they believe it? Which is why you need to get people both inspired and emotionally invested before you can influence their decision to embrace an otherwise otherworldly future. The story that people are interested in most is one that is somehow about *them*.

In 2018, Google presented its vision of the future at Google I/O annual developer conference. It unveiled its latest version of the Google Assistant technology. In the demonstration, CEO Sundar Pichai played a recording of Google Assistant independently calling a hair salon and booking an appointment. All by itself. According to a news report, "there was no hint of a robotic voice or that the salon employee recognized they were talking to AI."[9] This potential future is inspiring—and all about the consumers who will one day use it.

"Vision without execution is hallucination," Thomas Edison reportedly once said. All the vision in the world is nothing if it can't be turned into reality. That creative tension is the challenge we all face in overcoming disbelief and getting people to buy into the promise of what we're selling.

Now that you and your audience are on the same side regarding context and emotion, it's time to come back to the *data*. In this chapter, we're going to look at the supporting evidence—the data and proof—you will present to your audience so they can rationalize your big idea. You need to show that your story already exists with evidence of its truth. This is not make believe. You filter, envision, and bend the experience of reality through the stories you consume and create.

If you've told your *Undeniable Story* well so far, your audience wants your vision to prevail. They will be forgiving if your product is still a work in progress. All innovation is. After all, you are doing something that's never been done before! And despite your passion and belief, the truth is rarely self-evident.

"The truth
is rarely pure
and never
simple."

OSCAR WILDE

BASED ON A TRUE STORY

Our entire lives are built on stories. From the fairy tales our parents read to us as kids, to the history lessons we were taught in school, to the religious parables and family legends that taught us how to tell right from wrong in the world around us.

"The human species thinks in metaphors and learns through stories," said the anthropologist Mary Catherine Bateson. Here's the funny thing about stories. They're not truth. Not in the strictest sense. They're ephemeral. Stand-ins for reality. Yet, they are one of the most powerful ways to glimpse the deepest truths in life. Of course, discovering that a story is false or duplicitous can be one of the most shocking of betrayals. I learned this hard lesson when my zoo animal never materialized. The old Hollywood adage says it all: life is based on a true story.

Think of your favorite Academy Award–winning actors and actresses. Colin Firth as King George VI in *The King's Speech*. Reese Witherspoon as June Carter Cash in *Walk the Line*. Or Sean Penn as Harvey Milk in *Milk*. Each inhabits someone they are not so compellingly that their peers were moved to honor them for their performances. They are celebrated with an Academy Award for being the *best liars*. This puts a new spin on the idea and value of "make believe." Why do you watch a movie that you know isn't actually real? Because you accept the contract that comes with any good story. It's a reality simulator. Yet it better be relatable in order to keep you watching all the way through.

In much the same way, an *Undeniable Story* must be designed to overcome disbelief.

This is the biggest obstacle to disruptive innovation. And that's why I've been teaching you a range of storytelling strategies throughout this book. If you establish a compelling premise (context for change) along with characters and empathy (emotional dilemma), your audience will be practically begging you for the data (evidence of truth). They'll become a lot more forgiving about wherever you are in the journey to making your vision a reality. They'll see it as a journey they want to be a part of.

There are three questions your audience will ask about your story:

1   How do we know this story is true?
2   What gives you the right to tell us this story?
3   How can we trust and believe in the promise?

In this chapter, we'll explore some strategies for how you can (and should) assemble the evidence of truth that makes your story believable and credible.

HOW TO USE DATA TO SUPPORT YOUR PROMISE

In principle, every legal case is won or lost based on the supporting evidence. If the evidence is significantly in your favor and tangible in some way (for example, a written contract signed by both parties), you're likely to win the case. If your evidence is weak—or doesn't exist at all—chances are you're going to lose. Of course, there are other factors that influence a judge's or jury's decision, some of which are addressed in our early storytelling strategies related to context and emotion.

In much the same way, when telling your *Undeniable Story*, you need to present some kind of proof that shows your story is real and possible.

15 Sources of Evidence

1	Performance metrics	9	Testimonials
2	Personal story	10	Third-party endorsements
3	User research	11	Case studies
4	Scientific proof	12	Explainer video
5	Pilot projects	13	Communities
6	Historical precedent	14	Events and experiences
7	Product demos	15	Thought leadership
8	Customers		

Let's examine the 15 different sources of evidence.

1 **Performance metrics:** This is the most obvious—financial data and behavioral measures. Often you don't yet have metrics to share when you're on the front-end of innovation. Use this evidence to demonstrate positive signal and momentum toward future outcomes.

2 **Personal story:** This is a device on the other end of the spectrum. Share the origin story behind your quest—or a personal story that happened to you or to a customer—that symbolizes the dream, desire, and dilemma. Use this evidence to demonstrate intent, purpose, and motivation.

3 **User research:** This includes quantitative and qualitative research. Designed to bring you closer into the lives of those you want to serve. What do they want, need, or care about? Use this evidence to humanize the characters at the center of your story.

4 **Scientific proof:** This includes research studies, patents, algorithms, and the like. Anything that anchors your story in the scientific rigor of evaluation. Use this evidence to validate your underlying premise, technology, or differentiated position.

5 **Pilot projects:** This comprises initial betas, proof of concepts, and minimum viable products. A short sprint that demonstrates viability of demand and functionality. Use this evidence as proof that your vision is real and possible, at a small scale.

6 **Historical precedent:** Here you're using past milestones, breakthroughs, and progress in your respective category. The more precedent something has, the more real we perceive it to be. Use this evidence to establish a track record and demonstrate prior impact with the topic at hand.

7 **Product demos:** Here you offer an interactive demonstration of how it works. Give people a taste of what could be possible, moving from the abstract to the tangible. Use this evidence to make your message concrete, allowing your audience to experience your promise firsthand.

8 **Customers:** This category includes names, titles, logos, and headshots. Ideally feature individuals and brands that your audience admires, respects, and recognizes. Use this evidence to reinforce trust, relatability, and relevance—what you offer has been validated by others like them.

9 **Testimonials:** This includes written and video format from your users/customers/subject-matter experts. This is a way of having "other people" tell the story and affirm the good in what you're up to. Use this evidence to introduce a wider range of voices that validate your vision.

10 **Third-party endorsements:** Including awards, earned media coverage, and recognition. You're trading on the reputational,

celebrity, and trusted authority power of others. Use this evidence as a way to anchor the new into the familiar.

11 **Case studies:** This comprises stories and vignettes of past successes. Give your audience a way to envision the journey from initial need to ultimate outcome. Use this evidence to encourage your audience to identify with the journey as their own.

12 **Explainer video:** This is a short, one- to three-minute video. It illustrates what you do, who you serve, how it works, and why it matters. Use this evidence to demystify the complex.

13 **Communities:** This includes user forums, Facebook groups, email lists, and other social media channels. Anything that serves as a point of interaction where people can connect and express themselves on issues that matter. Use this evidence to demonstrate audience engagement and fandom.

14 **Events and experiences:** Including conferences, summits, and meetups. Designed to bring your ideas to life through face-to-face, real-world interaction. Use this evidence to demonstrate an active and engaged community with demonstrated shared interest and desire to build the future.

15 **Thought leadership:** This includes interviews, summits, books, white papers, and webinars. Create a content strategy that demonstrates depth of insight in a category. Use evidence to establish subject-matter expertise, authority, and commitment to your field.

STORYTELLING TIPS AND TRICKS

Truth is often in the eye of the beholder. It comes down to who is telling the story. Truth can be elusive and hard to pin down in black-and-white terms. There are often many shades of gray. Here are some tips to consider as you shape the evidence that will inform the truth at the heart of your *Undeniable Story*.

- **Still in startup.** What if you don't have enough data to prove your progress so far? Most innovators don't. You're doing something new and speculative. So, focus on other proof points, such as research that validates demand and unmet need. Or historical precedents and convergence of forces that legitimize the opportunity today.

- **Find a metaphor.** Comparables are a powerful way to show equivalency or comparison to an opportunity that has worked in other contexts. For example, "We're the Uber for recruiting"; "We're the WeWork for digital nomads"; "We're the Tinder for pets." (Yes, there is a Tinder for pets. In fact, several— Dog Date Afternoon and BarkBuddy to name just two.) Be careful, however, this strategy can become clichéd if it's overused.

- **Stories about social impact.** Tell a personal story about how one person's life has been changed, and then multiply it times the number of people served. You could say, for example, "This is the story of Elizabeth, and she is just one of the 3,000 lives that we transformed this past year." As neuroscientist Paul J. Zak reminds us, we need the personal human story to relate to before we can connect to the abstraction of a much bigger numbers.

- **Your narrative doesn't ring true.** Go back to Steps 1 (See It) and 2 (Feel It). When your narrative doesn't ring true, this speaks to a deeper fundamental misalignment and lack of relevance. Take a close look at how you've chosen to frame what you're doing and then rework it.

In this chapter, we explored the important role of truth in telling your stories and the three questions you need to answer for your audience. I showed you how to use data and evidence to prove that your *Undeniable Story* is real and possible. And I offered you some cautionary tales and tips to consider as you craft your own *Undeniable Story*.

Remember if you're not telling your story, somebody else is telling it for you.

It's up to you to tell your story—your *Undeniable Story*. With the tools you're learning in this chapter and in this book, you'll be able to do just that.

Consistently. Easily. Powerfully.

"The bad news, there
is no map. The
good news, you are
the map-maker."

———

ROSABETH MOSS KANTER

7

How to Build Narrative Intelligence

IN THIS CHAPTER

- Recap of the journey

- When to start a New Story

- How to lead the process

- Build organizational capability

- Embracing a storytelling walkabout

AS YOU MOVE forward with your own *Undeniable Story*, I would like you to keep the following key points from previous chapters in mind. They will serve as a guide, and I hope an inspiration, as you disrupt the world—and make it a better place for all of us.

In business, we all face three perceived limitations: (1) time, (2) money, and (3) people. However, when you align the forces of storytelling and innovation, you can stretch and defy these limitations—to bend the curve of history. With the right story—an *Undeniable Story*, one your audience cannot resist—you can 10x your performance.

You'll know your story is the right one when you can pass the 90 percent test—getting 90 percent of your audience on your side within five minutes. In my experience, the best way to do this is with a presentation that makes your audience feel good and creates a momentum of *yes*. If you want to transform how the world thinks about your product, cause, or message, focus on making people feel better about themselves.

You can craft your own *Undeniable Story* in just three steps:

STORY	NARRATIVE	STORY > NARRATIVE
Set-up	Context	Present the future in aspirational terms—how change leads to opportunity
Conflict	Emotion	Build empathy, describing the gap between desire and dilemma
Resolution	Evidence	Provide supporting data that legitimizes the promise of your big idea

CONTEXT

Business today is increasingly personal. When you know yourself, your stories telegraph your own values loud and clear. The heart of the storyteller becomes the heart of the story.

You can do this. The trick is to *think* in narrative. You're actually hardwired for it. The ability to make stories is quite literally a part of your DNA. Scientists have identified a specific gene, FOXP2, that they call the storytelling gene. You were born ready to story. So pay attention to the big picture and how you can frame your message in aspirational terms. Help people see the opportunities of tomorrow, today. What is worthy of elevation and celebration?

An effective storyteller takes the convergence of forces—technological, economic, and cultural—and puts it into a self-fulfilling context. How is the change you're describing an inevitable future, the natural direction of where the world is going, and how we can harness these forces for positive impact?

- **Technological forces:** hardware, software, interfaces, surfaces, bandwidth, etc.

- **Economic forces:** lower costs, more availability, change in supply/demand, etc.

- **Cultural forces:** new social values, emergent trends, redefinition of norms, etc.

EMOTION

Emotion is the fuel that propels your story forward. Neuro-economist Paul J. Zak discovered that classic storytelling structure generates a hormonal response: cortisol, then oxytocin. A classic tale captures your attention using a presenting drama or difficulty (cortisol). Then it concludes with a happy ending (oxytocin). You were introduced to the idea of reversing the order by which they are introduced. Based on the Feel-Good Principle, you want to start with oxytocin instead of cortisol. Information overload has put us increasingly in a fight/flight/freeze state. We need to break the cycle and ease back into a receptive state.

Other researchers have discovered that when people read stories, they build vivid mental simulations. Mirror neurons fire not only when *we* perform a particular action but also when we see *someone else* perform the very same action—whether in reality or through story.

We all have different neurological wiring, different life experiences, different perceptions of the world around us. Appreciate the differences: instead of trying to push your views onto your audience, welcome them into a new and exciting world.

When in doubt, make your customer the hero of the story. In the technology industry, there is a common habit of making the product or the brand the hero of the story, instead of a person. When you present a product as hero, you're focused on its amazing and remarkable features and benefits. Instead, the focus should be on the *user* of that product. What is that person trying to accomplish? What are the *jobs to be done*? What do they aspire to create or achieve through the use of this product? What are the frustrating obstacles that they keep coming up against? Where do they feel pain? How will this new thing help the user accomplish more and leap over the obstacles in their path?

EVIDENCE

When crafting an *Undeniable Story*, you need to present the proof that shows your story is real and possible. Demonstrate why you have the right to tell this story. Keep in mind that the truth is rarely pure or simple. It can be elusive and hard to pin down in black-and-white terms.

Creating an *Undeniable Story* means going deeper, looking farther, and expanding your vision of what's really possible. It means recognizing that story is not a thing, not a noun. Story is a process—it's a verb. And it's part of the continuum that is narrative. The goal is not only to think in narrative; it's to develop *narrative intelligence*.

THE PROCESS OF CREATING A NEW STORY

Now you've learned the basics of how to craft an *Undeniable Story*. This is a transformational framework to convey a bigger and better narrative about the future. That you can use anytime you need to inspire, influence, or innovate. To help others see the possibilities, opportunities, and potential that comes with disruptive change. Since this new approach may challenge old habits, give yourself the time to metabolize, test, and explore these methods. You may have experienced a few aha moments and insights along the way. Perhaps you're eager to share these insights with your coworkers, team members, and colleagues. Are you ready to create a New Story? We'll review that process together next.

In this final chapter, we'll answer these questions:

1   Where do you start if you want to change and craft a New Story?

2   How can you lead your company or team through a transformational story process?

3   What does it take to build storytelling as an organizational capability?

And we'll do that in practical terms with the following sections:

·   How to Start with Story
·   How to Lead a Story Sprint
·   Leadership Is Communication
·   Developing Narrative Intelligence
·   Putting Your Story into Practice

Let's go ahead and zoom back out to put your learnings into a broader context for action. How to apply what you've learned to the real world and seize the larger opportunities for next-level storytelling to transform your company, culture, or community.

"You've got to be able to communicate in life and it's enormously important ... If you can't communicate and talk to other people and get across your ideas, you're giving up your potential."

WARREN BUFFETT

HOW TO START WITH STORY

Remember that you came to this book with a vision, desire, or goal in your heart. A bigger story to tell. Get clear about your objective and desired outcomes. I encourage you to reconnect to your motivations and inspirations. Start with the story that's uniquely yours to tell.

Where do you have permission to craft and introduce a New Story? It depends on your role. Leverage your sphere of influence. If you're a CEO, you can start with the company-wide story. Otherwise, you may need to focus on your functional discipline, workstream, or initiative. What are the strategic priorities you need to deliver on in the next 12 months? Which of these areas would benefit from a stronger story and more compelling message? Where do you need to increase your ability to persuade, engage, and get buy-in from other stakeholders? Where does the current story feel stuck or lost in translation?

You have a story the world wants to know.
Here are a few potential threads of motivation:

- Reframe how you describe who you are, what you do, and why it matters

- Reposition your business and increase the perceived value of what you offer

- Lead business transformation and reimagine your customer experience

- Elevate the way your company thinks of design as a strategic imperative

- Raise millions of dollars or secure your next round of sponsorship

- Recruit and attract the best possible talent in a highly competitive market

- Inspire thousands of employees at the next company all-hands meeting

- Disrupt your category and want to redefine the game

- Change how your field talks about a specific cause or social issue

- Humanize a highly technical roadmap into a big-picture vision

- Be more confident when presenting in front of any audience

Quite simply, you want to get your story straight. It helps to have a meaningful motivation and reason for taking on the bigger story. This might not feel easy to choose, yet it's what determines everything. So get clear on why this matters. What's at stake is the essential first step in the process.

HOW TO LEAD A STORY SPRINT

Developing an *Undeniable Story* is a process you can start with your team in a half-day deep dive. Explore the ideas and exercises in this book. Or attend one of our workshops where we lead and facilitate this process for teams large and small, dozens of times every year. You need to start by first surfacing the elements of the story you have to work with.

Think of your story like Lego blocks. Ever give a box of Legos to a child? What's the first thing they build? Well, the picture on the box of course. It came with directions. Yet within a few days or weeks, a child gets bored. Or, better yet, inspired. And they want to create something new. So, what do they do? They take those Lego pieces and disassemble what they created. They throw the pieces to the ground. And build something new. That's how you need to approach your own *Undeniable Story* journey. Disassemble the Lego creation. Take inventory of what you have to work with. Then build something new. The exercises in See It, Feel It, and Believe It are designed to guide you in doing exactly that.

In our experience, phase 1 of creating an *Undeniable Story* takes at least 90 days.

In the first 30 days, you want to do *Story Discovery* with your team. Identify all the Lego pieces, clarify the vision vector, and name all the critical constraints and requirements. What does the narrative need to accomplish? Who does it need to speak to and why? And what's really on the line? Why do you need to get your story straight?

In the next 30 days, you move into *Story Design*: you build an outline of your *Undeniable Story*. You then begin to flesh it out with supporting details that color and animate the overall narrative: context, emotion, and evidence. A message map and storyboard help to organize all the different component pieces.

And in the last 30 days, *Story Development,* you focus on the creation of the final artifact or object that will bring the narrative to life. Usually, this is a slide deck presentation, a written narrative, or a video. Get clear on the use cases of where your *Undeniable Story* will be presented. Who needs to buy into and engage at different stages of the journey?

We recommend doing this 90-day process with a small working group, ideally three to five leaders who meet on a weekly basis. You can periodically bring a larger circle into the process at natural review points to gather input, validate assumptions, and create alignment.

In phase 2, it's time to work on the culture. This can easily last for three to nine months.

Your *Undeniable Story* is only as strong as the narrative is real to your customers, much less your sales team, cross-functional counterparts, and frontline employees. You can't just press send or publish and expect people to understand and embrace your story. Regardless of your stakeholders, channels, and touchpoints, you must invite people into the New Story. Give your audience the opportunity to experience and interact with the New Story. This is often done through town halls, all-hands meetings, summits, and workshops of various sorts. The key is to not just present the New Story but rather create an interactive format where people get to try on the story as their own. They get to discover and choose whether they belong in the New Story.

You also need to train your leaders in how to present the New Story. Ideally, this is individualized and brought to life through each person's own story. This is something that a few leaders naturally do; most others must be coached through the process. Once they get over the initial hump of fear and discomfort, leaders discover a whole new level of influence and confidence in how they connect with their people. You can make them true believers in no time.

In phase 3, you extend the story-making and culture-making process to defining rituals and experiences. This continues the journey of transformation over 18 to 24 months. From employee onboarding to customer hero stories to internal campaigns that bring your vision for the world to life. The beauty of great story-telling is that, when done right, it can become a never-ending story. As long as the world keeps changing, you'll keep having to change along with it. Which means there is always another chapter to be written. And a new fresh way to convey the promise of a new tomorrow.

To help you imagine the possibilities, examine the list of stories you can produce to 10x your results once the foundation of your *Undeniable Story* is established in the "Putting Your Story into Practice" sidebar.

LEADERSHIP IS COMMUNICATION

Being a great leader demands becoming a master communicator. The charisma to inspire and motivate people toward a brighter future. The skill to develop rapport and demonstrate empathy with anyone you meet. The willingness to be candid, transparent, and authentic. The agility to pivot in real time to the needs of your audience. To invite people to understand who you are and why you care. And from there invite people into a bigger version of the story and what's truly possible for them. What we can create or preserve together. This has been the role of the storyteller for thousands of years. It's just that the context and the stakes have changed dramatically.

This presents some unique challenges for organizations. You may have a handful of leaders who are natural-born storytellers and communicators. Who can intuitively connect the dots and humanize whatever subject is at hand. So, what do you do with everyone else? They may be highly competent managers who deliver strong business results with deep technical and analytical chops. Yet sometimes they're missing the emotional, relational, and communication skills required to lead people through change.

The future is a world where the half-life of change gets shorter and shorter. Where innovation becomes the ultimate survival of the fittest. Where managing volatility, uncertainty, complexity, and ambiguity (VUCA) is the new business as usual. Where artificial intelligence, machine learning, and big data are disrupting so many basic assumptions of life. Where the world of the future looks radically different than most of us can imagine, much less prepare for. That's the reality. And yes, we will adapt. Even to all this. Right now, the language of leadership is struggling to keep pace. We need a new vocabulary and a new set of tools for how we narrate and create the future.

This requires an evolutionary leap in storytelling. A new language and discourse for the age of disruption. Creating the future so many of us want to see realized. By harnessing the mindset, methods, and power of an *Undeniable Story*.

DEVELOPING NARRATIVE INTELLIGENCE

As we've explored, an *Undeniable Story* is not a one-off tale or anecdote. It's a new approach to storytelling. Focused on 10x thinking that leads to radical leaps and large-scale systemic transformation. The age of disruption was born from ingenuity and problem solving (the engineer), but as it matures, what it needs are more poets and creatives (the philosopher). We're all hungry

Putting Your Story into Practice

1 **Vision story > Aspiration**

Beyond strategy or OKRs. Bring the strategy to life, with a vector for where the world is headed. How can you turn this future into a self-fulfilling prophecy?

2 **Product story > Meaning**

Beyond the roadmap or feature stack. Humanize your product or solution in people's lives. How can you align stakeholders and get everyone emotionally invested?

3 **Customer story > Empathy**

Beyond just personas. Clarify who your story is for and how to make it relatable to them. What do they want, what gets in their way, and how are lives changed thanks to you?

4 **About story > Origins**

Beyond just history. Present your reason for being, humble beginnings, and your contributions to the greater culture. Why are you for real and to be trusted?

5 **Investor story > Opportunity**

Beyond just the slide deck. Describe the disruptive change, the opportunity market, and your solution. Why are you the team to make something happen?

6 **Brand story > Ethos**

Beyond just a tagline. Bring to life the promise, purpose, and values of your organization. The manifesto. Give people something to believe in. What does it feel like to be a part of this tribe?

7 **Marketing story > Campaign**

Beyond just go to market. Focus on the change you seek to create. What changes in emotions, beliefs, or behavior do you seek to create? And what stories can you serialize to make that true?

8 **Recruiting story > Talent**

Beyond the ordinary onboarding. Attract the right talent. How do you initiate them into the culture and how they can most meaningfully contribute?

9 **Culture story > Belonging**

Beyond a static mission and values statement. Put the brand and values into action. What are the stories that bring the ethos and message to life? What are the rituals of belonging?

10 **Thought Leadership story > Ideas**

Beyond a positioning statement. Share a unique point of view or expertise in your industry. How can you demonstrate your commitment to the future of your category?

for a more mature discourse with a focus on ethics, tradeoffs, and unintended consequences of how technology is reimaging and remaking the world.

What does this mean for you? Creating an *Undeniable Story* means going deeper, looking further, and expanding your vision of what's really possible. This bears repeating—recognize that story is not a thing, not a noun. Story is a process—it's a verb. And it's part of the continuum that is narrative. The goal is not just thinking in narrative; it's developing *narrative intelligence.*

We're all familiar with the ideas of cognitive intelligence (measured by IQ) and, more recently, emotional intelligence (measured by EQ). While IQ is believed to be relatively fixed over time, EQ can be improved through awareness and practice. Similarly, narrative intelligence—the innate human ability to make sense of, engage with, and connect with others—can also be improved through awareness and practice.

As business storytelling pioneer Steve Denning explains,

[Narrative intelligence] means the capacity to understand the world in narrative terms, to be familiar with the different components and dimensions of narratives, to know what different patterns of stories exist and which narrative patterns are most likely to have what effect in which situation. It also means knowing how to overcome the fundamental attribution error and understand the audience's story. It implies the ability to anticipate the dynamic factors that determine how the audience will react to a new story and whether a new story is likely to be generated in the mind of any particular audience by any particular communication tool.[10]

Narrative intelligence is two-way storytelling, which replaces the one-direction method of the past. It's the ultimate test of leadership to invoke inspiration, evoke emotion, and pivot to respond

"Intelligence is the ability to adapt to change."

STEPHEN HAWKING

"This is what we storytellers do. We restore order with imagination. We instill hope again and again and again."

WALT DISNEY IN *SAVING MR. BANKS*

to whatever the room or moment requires. Being present to what is and what could be is the artistry of the greatest leaders.

At Storied, we approach narrative intelligence as a developmental pathway.

Narrative intelligence has three components:

- **Mindset:** see possibilities amidst challenges and constraints

- **Methodologies:** know how to frame and reframe for resonance

- **Capabilities:** become the leader people want you to be

In this book, you've been introduced to the first two components, mindset and methodologies. Next-level leadership is a development pathway, from mindset and methodologies into capabilities. These capabilities are best summed up as embodied presence or inner capacity, along with a cultivated ability to communicate and connect in any situation from the mundane to the most demanding.

The ultimate goal then is how you can build storytelling as a capability.

What about robots and artificial intelligence? Won't they make the need for storytelling obsolete? It's quite the opposite. As more and more jobs become automated, the most important skills will be those of interpretation and meaning-making. What are the biggest limitations of AI at this time? Context and empathy. Notice the tie back to Step 1: See It and Step 2: Feel It. Our narrative abilities are what makes us most human. While you can teach a machine to *simulate* an understanding of nuance and caring, silicon chips aren't sentient beings. At least not yet.

It's consciousness—our ability to interpret complex and contradictory signals—that allows us to make meaning. That is the very thing that separates and defines us as a species. Which is why narrative intelligence will increasingly matter, more than ever.

While artificial intelligence will continue to remake much of modern life, narrative intelligence is what we desire most. Our humanity is built and sustained through narratives. Culture is a construct of meaning. And no matter how automated technology becomes, the human species is wired for making meaning. Which is why the data, the product, and the results never speak for themselves. *We* have to tell the story. Therefore, in the end, building narrative intelligence—within ourselves and our organizations—is a critical mandate of leadership. It is necessary to create the future we all desire.

A STORYTELLING WALKABOUT

In 2015, I became a global nomad. I sold most of what I owned and lived out of two carry-on bags for 500 days as I traveled

The Top 10 Skills of the Future

Take a look at the World Economic Forum's top 10 skills of the future (below).[11] You'll see that almost all of them fall under the broad umbrella of narrative intelligence. The set of interpretative and relational skills that allow us to thrive. Perhaps this is why a growing list of organizations recognize that storytelling needs to become an organizational capability.

IN 2020	IN 2015
1 Complex problem solving	1 Complex problem solving
2 Critical thinking	2 Coordinating with others
3 Creativity	3 People management
4 People management	4 Critical thinking
5 Coordinating with others	5 Negotiation
6 Emotional intelligence	6 Quality control
7 Judgment and decision making	7 Service orientation
8 Service orientation	8 Judgment and decision making
9 Negotiation	9 Active listening
10 Cognitive flexibility	10 Creativity

around the world. By one rationale, it was my dream deferred for 20-plus years. By another, I was recovering after a failed attempt to build StoryU, an online education platform devoted to teaching business storytelling. After going $250,000 in debt, and making every mistake in the playbook, we decided to pull the plug. It was time to empty the cup and recalibrate. I traveled and lived across 12 countries and four continents, delivering keynotes and storytelling workshops in Vancouver, Mumbai, Lisbon, Melbourne, Warsaw, London, New York, San Francisco, and countless other cities. All the while leading story sprints for our global clients in person and via video conference.

I was on a *walkabout* of sorts, conducting a global ethnography on storytelling, innovation, and culture-making. And rediscovering my true self in the process. We surround ourselves with things to tell the story of who we are. I was no different. It was a relief and delight to simply live off the presence of my being. I explored the spiritual storytelling traditions of India. I collaborated with the European innovation scenes of Amsterdam, London, and Lisbon. And I found my tribe in the design thinking communities of Australia. Each place I went, I learned about myself, our shared stories, and the universal themes of life. I also witnessed how, thanks to social media, my story existed outside myself. People would google me before we ever met in person. And they would experience my story in advance of my trip to their city. And in turn, I was welcomed with open arms. People would go out of their way to host me, friend me, and collaborate with me. This potential for familiarity is a gift of our age of inter-connectedness. Social media has democratized the storytelling process. Yet it doesn't happen unless you're willing to share your story and let yourself be seen.

As all the best stories go, I eventually fell in love, gobsmacked by the right woman. I landed back in the San Francisco Bay Area where I lived for two and a half years. Most recently, I moved back to Los Angeles in the summer of 2018, after being away for 25 years. As you might recall, Los Angeles is the land of my adolescence. Where I experienced the painful culture shock of being a Swiss boy in lederhosen and then an awkward American teenager who couldn't surf to save his life.

You could say we're all on a journey. All on the long walk home.

Everyone has a story. And everyone gets to tell their story. This book is just a thin slice of mine. Which I hope you've found parts of yourself in. Along with inspiration to help carry and articulate your own story of transformation out into the world. We live in truly remarkable times. Where we all get to story ourselves into being. No matter the stories of our past, we can reimagine, recreate, and reinvent a new future. This is your birthright! And the demands of the age we live in. The stories we tell literally make the world. If you want to change the world, you need to change your story.

The heart of the storyteller becomes the heart of the story.

"Words, in
my not so
humble opinion,
are the most
inexhaustible
source of magic."

———

PROFESSOR DUMBLEDORE

Bonus:
Digital Downloads

THANK YOU FOR buying this book.
   As a bonus, get access to additional storytelling resources:

- *Story 10x* case study examples
- Digital versions of the exercises in this book
- Discount to The New About Me, our bestselling e-course
- Free 10-part video series on telling a world-changing story
- Free storytelling toolkit for leaders of public libraries
- And more...

Visit **getstoried.com/Story10xBonus** and enter code: **bendthecurve**

Loved this book?
Post a review on Amazon.com or share on social **@getstoried** **#story10x**

We welcome your feedback and questions.
Email us at **story10x@getstoried.com**

For bulk order copies, email **books@getstoried.com**

Additional Resources

21 QUESTIONS FOR AN *UNDENIABLE STORY*

Step 1: See It—The Context for Change

1 Are you presenting change as a new opportunity and possibility?

2 Does the narrative describe a context that is relatable?

3 Is the narrative framed around a generally accepted truth?

4 Does the change effectively set up and legitimize your narrative?

5 What convergence of forces makes this narrative truer than ever before?

6 How is this narrative and the future it describes an inevitable conclusion?

Step 2: Feel It—The Emotional Dilemma

7 Who is at the center of the narrative (the hero or protagonist)?

8 What is their dilemma? Do you describe a clear desire versus an obstacle?

9 Will your audience identify and locate themselves in this story?

10 Does the dilemma present your protagonist in a dignified and respectful manner?

11 What is the heart of the story? Can your audience lean into it or do they look away?

12 What happens if they don't take advantage of this window of opportunity?

13 Who are the other characters that make the story meaningful?

Step 3: Believe It—The Evidence of Truth

14 How does your audience know this narrative is true?

15 What gives you the right to tell this narrative?

16 What proof can you provide to rationalize it?

17 What is the unique and distinctive way you address the dilemma?

18 What assets, learnings, and capabilities allow you to deliver on this promise?

19 How exactly does it work? What else does your audience need to know?

20 How are you inviting your audience to own and advance the narrative?

21 What are the next steps for people to get even closer to the narrative?

15 STORYTELLING AXIOMS

(From my book *Believe Me: A Storytelling Manifesto for Change-Makers and Innovators*)

1 People don't really buy a product, service, or idea: they buy the story that's attached to it.

2 Your brand is far more than just a name, a logo, or a tagline; it's the stories that people tell about you.

3 Every story exists in relationship to everything else around it.

4 We all want to look back at the story of our life and know that it made sense.

5 The stories we tell literally make our world.

6 The power of your story grows exponentially as more and more people accept your story as their truth.

7 If you want to learn about a culture, listen to the stories. If you want to change a culture, change the stories.

8 Leaders lead by telling stories that give others permission to lead, not follow.

9 Storytelling is our most basic technology, turbocharged through 21st-century innovation.

10 We all seek to experience our life in the most heroic of terms.

11 Nobody likes a change story, especially a change story that we have no control over. What people really need is a continuity story.

12 Our fate as a species is contained in the story. Both tyranny and freedom are constructed through well-supported narratives.

13 Storytelling empowers because it escapes the need to claim absolute truth.

14 Reinvention is the new storyline.

15 Storytelling is like fortune-telling. The act of choosing a certain story determines the probability of future outcomes.

Recommended Reading

WANT TO READ more of my work? You can find both of the following books on Amazon:

1 *Believe Me: A Storytelling Manifesto for Change-Makers and Innovators*
   If *Story 10x* is my first full-length studio album, then *Believe Me* is my original EP. It's a short, visually-driven book that serves as the perfect doorway and inspiration for anyone you want to introduce to the transformational power of storytelling.

2 *Wake Me Up When the Data Is Over: How Organizations Use Stories to Drive Results*, edited by Lori L. Silverman
   I'm a contributing author to this compendium on organizational storytelling, featuring 80-plus leading organizations. My chapter focuses on "turnaround stories"—how to reframe in difficult times. This is a resource for any of you who want to geek out on the history of the field of storytelling.

You'll find these books and more by going to **getstoried.com/ readinglist.**

- *All Marketers Are Liars* by Seth Godin

- *Building a StoryBrand: Clarify Your Message so Customers Will Listen* by Donald Miller

- *Circle of the 9 Muses: A Storytelling Field Guide for Innovators and Meaning Makers* by David Hutchens

- *Illuminate: Ignite Change through Speeches, Stories, Ceremonies, and Symbols* by Nancy Duarte and Patti Sanchez

- *Lead with a Story: A Guide to Crafting Business Narratives That Captivate, Convince, and Inspire* by Paul Smith

- *The Leader's Guide to Storytelling: Mastering the Art and Discipline of Business Narrative* by Steve Denning

- *Living Proof: Telling Your Story to Make a Difference* by John Capecci and Timothy Cage

- *Long Story Short: The Only Storytelling Guide You'll Ever Need* by Margot Leitman

- *Resonate: Present Visual Stories That Transform Audiences* by Nancy Duarte

- *Story: Substance, Structure, Style, and the Principles of Screenwriting* by Robert McKee

- *The Story Factor: Secrets of Influence from the Art of Storytelling* by Annette Simmons

- *Story Proof: The Science behind the Startling Power of Story* by Kendall Haven

- *Storyshowing: How to Stand Out from the Storytellers* by Sam Cawthorn

- *Story Smart: Using the Science of Story to Persuade, Influence, Inspire, and Teach* by Kendall Haven

- *The Storyteller's Secret: From TED Speakers to Business Legends, Why Some Ideas Catch On and Others Don't* by Carmine Gallo

- *Storytelling & the Art of Imagination* by Nancy Mellon

- *The Storytelling Animal: How Stories Make Us Human* by Jonathan Gottschall

- *Tell to Win: Connect, Persuade, and Triumph with the Hidden Power of Story* by Peter Guber

- *The User's Journey: Storymapping Products That People Love* by Donna Lichaw

- *Whoever Tells the Best Story Wins: How to Use Your Own Stories to Communicate with Power and Impact* by Annette Simmons

- *Winning the Story Wars: Why Those Who Tell (and Live) the Best Stories Will Rule the Future* by Jonah Sachs

- *Wired for Story: The Writer's Guide to Using Brain Science to Hook Readers from the Very First Sentence* by Lisa Cron

Acknowledgments

NO STORY is ever a straight line. It unfolds in twists and turns. Much of this book was written beside the Pacific Ocean at Sea Ranch Inn and finished in Culver City, CA. Many life shifts and transformations took place during this time.

Huge thanks to Jesse Finkelstein and the team at Page Two for your help in bringing my vision to life. My editing partners Peter Economy, Frances Peck, Crissy Calhoun, and Maggie Langrick. And the design vision of Peter Cocking and Taysia Louie, in collaboration with Jordan Short.

This book wouldn't exist without the tireless support and collaboration of my team at Storied. Jodi Bepler, your steady hand and smile forever means the world to me. Danielle Bennett, for all your meaningful contributions across the finish line. Angela Ekstowicz, Karoline Monkvik, and Gary Goldstein for all that you do. To my friends and colleagues, it takes a village: Sandra Wells, Tim Ogilvie, Christina Rasmussen, Pam Slim, Dan Mezick, and countless others.

My storytelling education was forever shaped at the feet of Paul Costello. Along with Madelyn Blair, Seth Kahan, Alicia Korten, Steve Denning, and the GoldenFleece storytelling community of practice. Also, I'm forever in gratitude to Desda Zuckerman, David Kitts, and the CI community for my most heartfelt lessons on the path of transformation.

A deep bow of thanks to my mom, Leslie, and dad, Geoff, whose creative mojo and work ethic continue to inspire me to this day. It feels so good to be back home in Los Angeles. Our regular Monday night dinners are my favorite night of the week.

At the end of the day, the best stories are always a love story.

Notes

1 Howard Schultz and Dori Jones Yang, *Pour Your Heart Into It: How Starbucks Built a Company One Cup at a Time* (Hachette, 1997), p. 79.

2 Seth Godin, "Creating stories that resonate," Seths.blog, August 20, 2008, seths.blog/2008/08/creating-storie.

3 Comment by Jim Signorelli on Michael Margolis, "You are a storyteller, and you have a story worth telling," GetStoried .com, getstoried.com/storyteller-story-worth-telling, posted on August 29, 2014.

4 Chelsi Nakano, "[Infographic] The 2018 state of attention," Prezi Blog, August 28, 2018, blog.prezi.com/the-state-of-attention-2018-infographic.

5 Lisa Cron, *Wired for Story: The Writer's Guide to Using Brain Science to Hook Readers from the Very First Sentence* (Ten Speed Press, 2012), p. 67.

6 Chris Ziegler, "Nokia CEO Stephen Elop rallies troops in brutally honest 'burning platform' memo? (update: it's real!)," *Engadget*, February 8, 2011, engadget.com/2011/02/08/nokia-ceo-stephen-elop-rallies-troops-in-brutally-honest-burnin.

7 Lisa Cron, *Wired for Story: The Writer's Guide to Using Brain Science to Hook Readers from the Very First Sentence* (Ten Speed Press, 2012), p. 107

8 Stephen Karpman, "Fairy tales and script drama analysis," karpmandramatriangle.com/pdf/DramaTriangle.pdf.

9 Chris Welch, "The 10 biggest announcements from Google I/O 2018," *The Verge*, May 8, 2018, theverge.com/2018/5/8/17328828/google-io-keynote-summary-highlights-news-recap-2018.

10 Steve Denning, "Beyond storytelling: narrative intelligence." SteveDenning.com, 2016. stevedenning.com/Language-of-Leadership/narrative-intelligence.aspx.

11 Alex Gray, "The 10 skills you need to thrive in the Fourth Industrial Revolution," *World Economic Forum*, January 19, 2016, weforum.org/agenda/2016/01/the-10-skills-you-need-to-thrive-in-the-fourth-industrial-revolution/.

About the Author

MICHAEL MARGOLIS is the CEO and founder of Storied, a strategic messaging firm specializing in the story of innovation and disruption. As a trusted advisor, Michael helps executives to demystify the complex and deliver on the promise of transformation. Michael operates anywhere there is a story worth telling, especially in Silicon Valley, Fortune 500s, and global change. Michael is a frequent keynote speaker at top conferences around the world. He's trained tens of thousands on narrative intelligence and how to build storytelling as an organizational capability. Michael partners with C-suite executives, along with heads of product, design, marketing, community, and human resources. Since 2002, he's advised clients across 34 industries and 15 countries—including Facebook, Google, Hulu, Greenpeace, and NASA.

Michael is a two-time TEDx speaker, number-one Amazon bestselling author, and has more than 200,000 followers on Twitter. His work has been prominently featured in *Fast Company*, *TIME*, and *Inc.* magazines. Armed with a degree in cultural anthropology, Michael began his career as a social entrepreneur, funded by the Ford and Rockefeller Foundations by the age of 23.

And became a startup-failure by the age of 24. The son of an inventor and artist, Michael grew up in Switzerland and Los Angeles. As a passion project, Michael recently cofounded Choco Libre, a secret society devoted to rare and exotic craft chocolate. Michael is left-handed, color-blind, and eats more chocolate than the average human.

- To book Michael for a keynote, email **jodi@getstoried.com**

- For media requests, email **danielle@getstoried.com**

- For bulk order copies, email **books@getstoried.com**

About Storied

STORIED is a strategic messaging firm. With a specialty for telling the story of innovation and disruption. As trusted advisors, we demystify the complex and support you on the journey of business transformation. We operate anywhere there is a story worth telling, especially in Silicon Valley, Fortune 500s, venture-backed startups, and global changemaking organizations.

Crafting Strategic Narratives

We build narratives for your most important priorities and initiatives:

- Executive Comms
- Corporate Vision & Strategy
- Investor Fundraising
- Brand Storytelling
- Business Transformation
- Employer Branding
- Change Management
- Summits & All-Hands

We partner with C-suite executives, along with heads of product, design, marketing, community, and human resources. Perhaps you are working on an ambitious future that is hard to describe or convey. You are seeking to humanize and simplify the technical.

You are challenging the status quo and redefining the future of your industry. That's where we come in.

Building Storytelling as an Organizational Capability

For over 15-plus years, we have created impact for hundreds of clients including Google, Facebook, Uber, Hulu, Slack, InVision, Genentech, NBC Universal, American Express, Bloomberg, Deloitte, EY, Northwestern Mutual, AARP, American Library Association, Robert Wood Johnson Foundation, The Nature Conservancy, Greenpeace, UN Foundation, Zappos, and NASA.

We'd love to teach you our methods. We deliver dozens of top-rated storytelling training programs around the world every year. Our narrative trainings are especially for managers that need to inspire, influence, and lead transformation. We also partner with leaders who want to bring their vision, strategy, and people into cohesive alignment.

Visit **getstoried.com** to get started.